MR.
PO B
HEPBURN SK S0K 1Z0

S0-EKO-386

Second Thoughts

Katie Funk Wiebe

KINDRED PRESS
Hillsboro, Kansas
1981

SECOND THOUGHTS

Copyright © 1981 by Kindred Press, Hillsboro, Kansas 67063

All rights reserved. With exception of brief excerpts for review, no part of this book may be reproduced without the written permission of the publisher.

Library of Congress Catalog Card Number: 81-80122
International Standard Book Number: 0-937364-01-0

Printed in the United States of America

Cover design by Duane Penner

Printing by Mennonite Brethren Publishing House
Hillsboro, Kansas 67063

*To all those friends
who keep encouraging me to write
and believe that I can*

Table of contents

Introduction

Over the years I have admired the way Katie Funk Wiebe gets at the nitty-gritty issues of life. And I am always amazed at her productivity. She is one of the most creative writers in dealing with issues which must be dealt with in the Christian life and I always come away from reading her articles and columns with fresh insight. She forces me to face again what I believe and stretches my mind and spirit. I like that in an author and in this volume she does it chapter after chapter.

In *Second Thoughts* Katie Funk Wiebe disturbs what needs to be disturbed — our religiosity, our Christianity, and our Laodicean lukewarmness. The secret of her effectiveness is not in telling us what or how we ought to change. Instead she shares what God and others share with her, how her own perceptions change and what is happening in her own inner life and commitments. Further, we sense her deep love for the church. This love leads her to lift before us subtle flaws which all of us can see in ourselves, but which often go unnoticed. And she does it in order that we may be nudged nearer the Christ-life in all our relationships.

By the way Wiebe identifies with us in a sympathetic and caring spirit she continues to draw our attention and admiration. We see ourselves in her struggles, desires and aspirations.

Don't read this book if you are unwilling to change, adjust or to grow. But if you want to move beyond where you are at this moment, read a chapter and take time to ponder what it says and involves before moving to the next. These short chapters will nurture while they needle. They will search the heart while they stretch the mind. They will call to new commitment while they challenge old conclusions. And that is what is necessary to grow.

Who should read this book? If you are a Christian — young or old, you will profit from it. I see these chapters forming a daily reading series for persons who desire spiritual stimulation, strength and sustenance beyond the pablum level of many devotional books. Here are truths and ideas worthy of devotion in the truest sense.

I can see these chapters as excellent stimulators for discussion in all kinds of small groups, including Sunday school classes.

I wish every church leader would take time to read *Second Thoughts*. These chapters might well be solid diet for a pastor's own devotional life. Many of these chapters could form input for congregational or denominational board meetings and committees. Here all church leaders will gain a good perspective on the essence and essentials of church life as well as a challenge to individual commitment to discipleship.

I enjoyed reading *Second Thoughts* and I plan to return to it again and again. I predict others will do the same.

> *John Drescher*
> *Eastern Mennonite College*
> *Harrisonburg, Virginia*

Author's preface

I talk to people. I talk to God. I talk to myself. Sometimes the conversation with myself isn't very long, deep or even mannerly. Usually it is about something that bothers me. Then, after I've had time for reflection and study, I put my second thoughts about the subject of conversation on paper.

As I write I see people, who like myself, are sometimes elated, sometimes perplexed, sometimes concerned and sometimes assured about the Christian life and the church. I know the more personal an experience or feeling is, the more likely it is to be universal. I also see people who are looking for assurance from someone that their feelings are shared by others.

The writer who helps me most is not the one who tells me what I already know and believe or what I should know and believe, but the one who states clearly the concerns I have been struggling to express. In these second thoughts, I attempt to articulate for readers the puzzlements, joys and concerns we share about life.

I acknowledge my debt to writers like A. W. Tozer, Oswald Chambers, Elton Trueblood, Elizabeth O'Connor and others who have shaped my thinking about the Christian walk. I recognize that their first thoughts are part of my second thoughts. I repay my debt to them by drawing their thinking to your attention, certain that if we keep talking about important truths of God, you will meet them again, and so will I. To keep quiet means that these truths take on a pedestrian pace and get shoved into oblivion.

Columnist Art Buchwald pokes fun for a living. Jack Anderson digs dirt. Ann Landers gives advice. And Sylvia Porter keeps people solvent. My task is to keep us from getting too comfortable in our cushioned pews. The writings in this book, most of which have been published in some form previously, represent a cross section of my searchings for truth, changes in my thinking, and my affirmations about Christ and the church. I offer them to you with the hope they will cause you to have second thoughts about them.

Katie Funk Wiebe
Hillsboro, Kansas
January 1981

. . . about
the quest
for the
faith-life

God is for real

1

You: *Isn't it sort of strange to be talking to yourself?*

Katie: *Not really — I do it all the time. Everytime an idea knocks at the door of my mind, I have a little chat with it first before I let it in — if I let it in.*

You: *What have you been talking to yourself about recently?*

Katie: *Lots of things. For instance, people keep mentioning having a "personal relationship with Christ."*

You: *What other kinds of relationships could a person have? An impersonal one?*

Katie: *That's not the issue. Some people keep saying Christ is real to them, but I wonder if they know what they're saying.*

You: *Are you saying the phrase is just a fad, like—*

Katie: *Not exactly a fad. The Apostle Paul said, "I know whom I have believed." He didn't talk about a personal relationship, yet what did he mean by his words "knowing Christ"?*

Look at this! Three thousand dollars for a first-person account of an outstanding spiritual experience. What an easy way to get rich! You don't even have to know how to write. Just have the experience and someone else will write it up for you, the article says.

But what if you haven't had the experience to write about? What if you haven't had a dramatic turning point in life or a miraculous answer to prayer that makes a good story?

That's the problem.

Admittedly, the religious experience of many Christians has been just a tiny upheaval, like a tired puff of wind on a hot summer day. They wish desperately there were some way of damming up the Holy Spirit for a few minutes — even for half an hour. Then, maybe, they might be able to have a real winner of an experience — not to sell for money or to have something to say at a testimony meeting — but simply because God would then be alive to them — a real person.

That's what they want. To know God. They have this hunger inside and also the tiny doubt that unless they can talk about some dramatic moment when Christ appeared before them bathed in light that Christianity may be some preacher's smokescreen to keep the people placated.

Most Christians have been taught as children that God is a person, must be accepted as a person, and can be known as a person. Yet how many know him as they know husband or wife, child or parent? What does Billy Graham or any other preacher mean when he says a Christian can have a personal relationship with Christ?

According to the late A. W. Tozer, God is nothing more than an inference or a deduction for most non-Christians. If they believe in God, they may think of him as an ideal or as the symbol of goodness, beauty, truth or love. However, writes Tozer, even though most Christians agree that God has a personality and can be known as a person, he is no more real to them than he is for the non-Christian. He remains something vague and distant.

For many believers, Christ is the one they accepted as Savior, but this "personal relationship" aspect is an empty set of words to them. They would like to have a relationship with him, but they don't know what they have to do to get the experience that will make Christ real. They think about the idea of God in odd moments, but beyond that, God is no closer than the friend living 500 or 5,000 miles away, and their prayers bring him no closer.

How do you know God? Is he real or only imagined? What does the reality of God depend on?

I am glad the reality of God doesn't depend on what I believe about him. That would mean that when my faith is weak, I'd snuff out his life. Puff — and he'd be gone! God has existence as a Spirit endowed with a personality apart from anything I choose to believe about him. The Bible says so.

God exists just as the typewriter on which I am typing this manuscript exists and functions as a typewriter — whether or not *I believe* it is real. My perception of this machine does not alter the fact of its existence or purpose.

I am glad that God can be known by human beings. "They that seek me, shall find me," said Christ. Just as I always know if I have found what I am looking for, whether it is a pair of scissors or my car in the shopping plaza parking lot, I can also know when I have found Christ.

If it is possible to find and to know Christ, then we human beings must have faculties whereby it is possible to do so. These faculties, used far too little, are spiritual and are brought to life through the new birth. "He that comes to God must believe that he is and that he is a rewarder of them that diligently seek him."

But I'm human. I like to feel warm arms reaching around me and holding me and a voice that speaks audibly and tells me I'm okay. How can I know God is real? I can't see him. I can't reach out and touch him. I can't hear his voice.

True, I may not be able to feel and to hear him, but I know him because he has given me an inner consciousness of himself. I hear his voice speaking to my spirit when I become quiet. Often it is through his Word. I feel the strength of his arms supporting my spirit in the way a parent carries a weary child.

Sometimes the arms and voice are those of another Christian and the words are their Spirit-directed words. The reality of Christ is grasped by the Spirit in me. It requires the leap of faith.

If our search for Christ is for a mind-boggling experience, we will miss both it and Christ. If we are searching for God, we will know when we have found him.

Please say the magic words for me

2

Katie: *Surgery? That'll mean almost two months of the summer wiped out. Why did God let me get sick again?*

You: *Why not pray to God for instant healing? You need to stay at your work to support the family. The kids need you healthy. God has promised to be with widows and orphans in their affliction. I think I can find a verse to prove this.*

Katie: *But does that verse mean — instant relief?*

You: *If it doesn't, why is it in the Bible? What else could it mean? After all, what's a God for?*

Few Christians pass through life without wishing, at one time or another, consciously or unconsciously, they could invoke a magic power to come to their aid. Some call this power God.

A child or other loved one lies seriously ill. A difficult decision must be made regarding one's job or business. Son or daughter hasn't caught on what life is about and keeps messing it up. Maybe even a favorite football team keeps losing. And the preacher hasn't said anything new in six months.

If only one knew a few magic words! Presto! The world would again be the way we want it — good health, clean-cut decisions, interesting sermons and obedient children. If only God could be persuaded to perform every day as he did for Gideon in the Old Testament. All one would have to do is put out a fleece each evening along with the cat. In the morning, the answer could be picked up with the newspaper and put into action.

As a child, I shared with other youngsters in the community an uneasy, if superficial, belief in superstition, ghosts and magic. By avoiding black cats, the number thirteen, beginning a journey on Friday, we hoped happiness and success would be our lot. Most persons drop such superstitions after adolescence; a few carry them over into adult life, Christians included.

Without actually wanting to, a person may slip into a pattern of belief which attributes spiritual power or value to material objects, to the recitation of certain words, to carrying specific objects or to undertaking ritual actions — all in the hope that a higher power can be persuaded to act on one's behalf.

The Jewish leaders fell into this habit. God had commanded them to wear selected passages of Scripture upon their person to remind them of their responsibility to obey the Word and to love the Lord above all. By the time of Christ this practice had degenerated into pure superstition. The phylacteries in which the Scriptures were carried had taken on magical qualities and were considered a source of power in and of themselves.

The Christian church has few sacred objects, such as phylacteries, which can be endowed with supernatural power, yet this does not put its members out of danger. Because of the high value the church places on the Bible as the Word of God, it is in danger of making the Scriptures a magic book and Christianity mechanical and artificial. The right procedures will bring the desired results.

Former missionary Anna B. Mow tells the story of a Moslem woman who was asked to heal a sick child. She wrote a verse of the Koran on paper, put the paper in a glass of water and gave it to the mother of the sick child with the instructions that the youngster drink the liquid in which the ink had dissolved to get the full benefit of the power of the Word. Mrs.

Mow mentions another woman in India who used the Bible as a charm and felt insecure if it fell out of her grasp at any time. Her faith was in possessing the book physically, not in grasping the meaning of its words.

I once knew a woman, a sincere Christian, who came to regard the Bible in what seemed to me a similar way. If she didn't know which direction the cows had headed at milking time, she opened the Bible at random, stuck her forefinger on a verse, and looked for wisdom about the ways of errant cows in that portion of Scripture.

We don't dissolve religious words in water or play Bible roulette, yet some Christians believe that a Scripture verse attached to any object, however trivial, gives that object greater value. A letter opener, a pencil, or a ruler seems more worthy as a gift if it has "The Lord is my shepherd" parading down the side or back.

During a lengthy illness, I became aware of the pressure of radio and television preachers on listeners to write for semi-religious objects, such as a mustard seed encased in plastic to be worn as a bracelet charm, or an illuminated cross, to make their faith more meaningful. In what way, I ask.

Or consider the numbers of people who feel uncomfortable without a Bible in their home, preferably in full view on the coffee table, but who never read it. Its presence, rather than its meaning, gives them security.

Then there are those who want the benefits of a close relationship with God but don't want the relationship itself, because like any relationship, it takes time and effort to develop. One of the most difficult activities to fit into today's hurried spectator-oriented life is time for private worship. When does one pray, if at all? Before one goes to the ball game? Or after watching the late movie? Prayer and the late news don't fit too well either. Sometimes prayer seems like an anachronism left over from the period of hand-cranked cars and high-buttoned shoes.

Plain, old-fashioned prayer doesn't work fast enough for

today's generation, anxious for quick results. Some persons get turned off by the neat little thoughts in devotional books, which are often better exercises in wit and alliteration than in the work of the Holy Spirit. For others, prayer isn't fulfilling what they have been taught about it (God answers prayer), so after keeping up the forms for a while, they become disillusioned and drop the whole matter. But they wouldn't mind a little magic from God in a pinch.

In the ancient Greek theater when one of the mortal characters got into a particularly tight spot, a god appeared abruptly to help him out of his dilemma. This god was lowered to the stage from a machine or stage structure, as needed, and became known as a *deus ex machina*.

Who hasn't prayed for help or wisdom at a critical moment, and then waited in impatient agony for God to step down from his heavenly throne and wave a big STOP or GO sign, like a flagman on the highway, forcing us to take the new way? We want to be spared the pain of deciding the next step.

And that's the reason we want magic. It's more convenient and means less responsibility on our part. And less pain.

The Christian life is a meaningful relationship between a personal God and the person who chooses to follow him. It is not a magical connection dependent on knowing the right words or owning the right book. To use God-words like magic words is an attempt to manipulate God and constitutes a return to paganism. The life of faith is an intelligent relationship with **God based on trust and an understanding of his Word. To memorize prooftexts is not enough. To hold a gilt-edged leather-bound Bible is not enough. Studying the Word is a beginning.**

3

Katie: *I'm too tired tonight to read the Bible or pray, so good-night.*

You: *But you were too tired last night also — don't you remember? And the night before —*

Katie: *Yeah, sure, so what? Can I help it? The church expects me to keep running to its meetings night after night, and then I've got to prepare lectures for tomorrow's classes — and then my editor expects a nice-sounding article by Monday morning.*

You: *That's right. Tell it like it is! People expect too much of you. Extra stuff like prayer should not be required of a busy Christian.*

"Ten days in isolation in the cells." The sentence is swift and cruel for a seemingly slight offense.

The scene is from the film "One Day in the Life of Ivan Denisovich," based on the book by Alexander Solzhenitsyn, the exiled Russian writer. One of the prisoners in the concentration camp is being punished. His crime? He had somehow acquired and worn an extra undershirt while working in the bitter cold of the Siberian tundra. No prisoner is allowed more than the thin, inadequate regulation clothing.

As the offender is led out, a fellow prisoner comforts him

with "At least you will have time to think." Each moment of
each day of each year of each long prison sentence of each
prisoner has to be accounted for to some authority. Time to
meditate is a forbidden luxury.

As I watched this gripping film, I wondered whether
people today long for time to be alone. Do they even need time
to meditate? Has meditating become an old-fashioned activity
which went out with lawn croquet and the Victrola?

As I watch the Christian community bustle about like a
barnyard full of chickens on a sunny day, I wonder when these
people take time for reflection upon the Word of God. Possibly
many read the Bible, but that is not meditation. The two are
not synonymous. Yet if Christians no longer find meditation
profitable, does it make any difference to their lives or to the
growth of the church? When the going gets rough, does their
faith disintegrate like an overused paper towel, or does it show
strength?

The presence or absence of meditation on the Word of God
in the life of a Christian makes a difference, say some Christian
thinkers. The extent to which the Christian neglects such
nurture is the extent to which worldliness reigns in that person.
Meditation means God's truths become our reference points
throughout the day. No meditation means other factors become
our reference points and keeps our day in line with reality.

Is this your day? The clock-radio alarm goes off and the
news and weather come on. The newspaper is scanned over the
last cup of coffee at breakfast. Then work. All day. The evening
news is the appetizer before supper and the late news and a talk
show the nightcap.

Surely to get most of our insights and ideas for our
thought-life from newspapers, radio and television, and to get
our Bible truths only from snippets of discussion and a weekly
20-minute sermon leaves our value system open to manipulation by what have become the real reference points each day —
the news, sportscasts, morning paper and coffee breaks. These

opinion makers define for us what is important and determine our needs, ideas and ambitions.

Most people have some fairly good reasons why they don't spend more time in meditation. Some are disenchanted with a devotional life because in earlier years, when it was forced on them, it led only to spiritual navel-gazing and not to involvement with the real needs of others. At a time when social justice is a growing concern, private meditation seems a dead end. Today it is important to *do* rather than to *be*. Our age has become increasingly suspicious of mental activity while reinforcing other kinds of activity. If a Christian is not out "doing," he or she is backsliding. Activity is associated with life (and relevance), while inactivity is associated with death (and irrelevance).

The older I grow the more complex life becomes and the more convinced I am that every Christian needs time for reflection. Unless our lives are shaped from within by the working of the Spirit of Christ through the Word, we easily get swept into the crowd on the broad way.

In this fast-paced world I need time to sort things in my mind. Each day I face new issues relating to family, church and community. I also have to cope with the pressures of daily life and work, which doesn't often leave time for an activity which has few measurable results. Plain weariness from the activities of the day, some good and productive in themselves, make the temptation to relax a pleasant invitation. Who wants to spend time rethinking a rotten day?

I got some help from Paul Tournier's *Fatigue in Modern Society*. He relates how at one period in his life he was much involved in church activities, but inwardly empty. As a theologian, he found it easy to work with ideas about God. He could work out twenty sermons on a Scripture text, yet he had no contact with God.

He dates his personal renewal to the time he made room for meditation in his daily schedule. He makes the distinction

between meditation and Bible study. He wasn't always successful in maintaining his new schedule, but he concludes that the
Christian needs to "proclaim the value of meditation . . . because
all great reform begins with the inner man . . . even while
admitting personal inadequacies."

Ten days in isolation? Would it be punishment or a
blessing in disguise if someone meted that sentence out to you?

Modern
blindness

4

You: *Hey, shouldn't you say something to the person next to you about the difference Christ could make in her life? Look at her! She's reading some trashy magazine. Pull out your Bible and read it in full view of her.*

Katie: *What should I say? What difference does Christ make in my life? I see as many happy non-Christians as Christians. That bothers me.*

You: *But they couldn't really be happy without Christ, could they?*

Katie: *I'm not so sure — I think she's going to talk to me — what'll I say? What'll I say to her?*

Sometimes I ask my fellow Christians why we should bother people with the good news about Jesus Christ. Happiness is not an answer. Many non-believers are happy, satisfied, have a good self-image, a sense of purpose and live fulfilled, moral lives. A promise of a future heaven or hell is not an answer either. Many people have discarded such notions years ago with trikes and sandboxes.

My question may seem foolish, but the vague answers I receive justify it. They are good for filling in the blanks of a workbook, but not for real life. If these people believed what they said, they'd be more concerned with their neighbor's soul than with the scratch he made on the fender of their station wagon when he backed out of the driveway last Monday.

Certainly we'd have to agree that some non-Christians are happy and working effectively for the betterment of human-kind, sometimes more successfully than Christians. And some of both kinds are unhappy, poorly adjusted to life and live mostly for themselves. If there is little visible difference in the lives of a Christian and a non-Christian, except for their Sunday morning habits, why get excited about the gospel? What difference does living for Christ make in a person's life?

Something valuable has left the body of Christ if its members can't decide what a person would gain by joining their fellowship other than acquiring a new set of activities and possibly a new group of friends.

J. B. Phillips in *Ring of Truth* says there is so little difference between Christians and their unbelieving neighbors because they have lost their enthusiasm for the gospel. Christians today think quite differently about God than did Paul and Peter and their contemporaries. These men had experienced the invasion of God in their lives. Christ had come to live in them and changed their purpose and pattern of living.

Christians today do not seriously believe that God is willing to enter a human life and transform it. Members of Alcoholics Anonymous and similar organizations show more faith in a power greater than themselves than many Christians evidence in God. Members of AA also realize they need one another to kick their drinking habit. Not all Christians would admit they need other members of the body of Christ to help them get rid of covetousness, gluttony, or to remain courageous in the face of adversity.

The God some Christians believe in today is a faraway God. They keep him at arm's length at the end of a leash like a pet dog. They take him out to church on Sunday, or occasional-ly walking on weekdays, but also feel free to discard him like an empty can when they no longer need him. He is extra to their lives, not central.

According to Phillips, a second blindness of modern Christians is an unwillingness to believe that the powers of evil are real and in opposition to the will of God. Sin mysteriously left the Christian's life when it left the working vocabulary of society as a whole. Today people rarely sin. They make goofs, errors, mistakes, bloopers, but never commit sins against God. Seldom does one hear of Christians struggling with sin in their daily life, and non-Christians never do. To battle sin seems unsophisticated, and to admit weaknesses and problems suggests unspirituality. Persons who are on their way up or who have already arrived in church circles don't do such things. One must always negotiate from the position of strength, not weakness.

When God invades a life, the struggle with the forces of evil does not end. Sometimes it only begins. It may mean that questions will increase and the answers seem less platitudinous. It will be a struggle the Christian is aware of. Phillips says that "it is only when we are going in the same direction as the devil that we are unconscious of opposition."

We have little to tell our non-Christian friends when we are blind to the fact that the Christian life is a glorious, but temporary, pilgrimage with God to a life to come. We have little to say when we have become settlers instead of remaining pilgrims. We have little to say when we are no longer daring adventurers for God ready to risk all for his sake. We have little to say when we have become humanists with a slight tinge of Christian piety.

To be on a personal journey with Christ, both inward and outward, is important to be a true witness. The person who merely talks about it but doesn't live it has few listeners. The person who doesn't live it has nothing to talk about.

Life is for living

5

Katie: *A lot of people run around with a low sense of self-esteem. I hear too few people say they feel confident about themselves and their work.*

You: *It could be their upbringing. I grew up thinking I shouldn't think much of myself.*

Katie: *But if you hated yourself, wouldn't that mean also hating the Christ dwelling in you? Wouldn't you also be keeping him from revealing himself to others?*

While waiting recently in the lobby of a large public lounge, I noticed a large modern iron sculpture, about eight feet high, near the window. Hundreds of pieces of iron of all shapes and sizes had been painstakingly welded together and overlaid with gold and black paint in an abstract design.

"What is it supposed to say?" I asked myself, as my eyes wandered up and down the curves and corners, trying to find the key which would unlock its significance. I found none. The welded pieces remained a mass of cast iron.

Then I chuckled. What if the creator of this massive object had intended it to have no meaning? Maybe he just made something to fill up space in a lounge. If so, was the joke on him or on me?

The question about meaning and significance troubles many people as they wait in the lobbies and waiting rooms of

18

life looking at the bits and pieces of their lives. The young perched on the edge of adulthood ask the question as do the old living on the waning edge. Sick, well, poor, rich, oppressed, free — no one is exempt.

For some people the question arises out of a concern that life has meaning but it has bypassed them. For others, it is a morbid concern. They fear life may have no real meaning. They fear that human beings are only objects to fill space — nothing but a flesh and blood machine, predetermined by environment and heredity, set in motion until the life spring runs down and the body is buried six feet underground.

Persons like rock singer Janis Joplin questioned the significance of life. She made her decision with an overdose of drugs. Yet some young people who would never go to such extremes ask her question also. What discomfits them — and us — is that they are Christians, raised in Christian homes; they have passed through twelve to fifteen years of Sunday school, church and youth fellowships.

Doubtless our fast-paced world and the depersonalizing effects of technology, mass education and increasing violence make life seem empty, brutal and mechanical. Yet meaning has departed from the ranks of the saints for other reasons. In the church we are guilty of explaining and simplifying and trying to make the gospel so comfortable and familiar to God-seekers, there is nothing left for them to seek and find. We have hammered and molded and routinized the faith into a shape which can be easily handled, recognized and even advertised, so that the mystery of the Cross and the sense of awe at the mysterious workings of God in the life of a believer are shunted aside.

Second, we have stressed too much that life is for dying instead of for living, and inadvertently preached a theology of meaninglessness. I went through young adulthood believing that it was scriptural to hate oneself, that it was necessary to die to self and to become a "nothing" so that Christ could become a "something." "Self" and "life" became dirty words. I

watched Christians struggle toward the goal of becoming
"channels only," "instruments" and "meek, insignificant
worms like Jacob." The process of dying included refusing
invitations to serve in church work in which one might receive
public attention, never openly acknowledging one's gifts or
volunteering to help in an area one felt competent to serve.
Above all, compliments were rejected. Pride was the most
heinous sin.

It is true that Scripture teaches death to sin and self, but it
also teaches being alive to God. Christ said many things about
self and the quality of life on this earth (Mt. 16:24-28 *NEB*).
Paul assured the Ephesians that life has purpose (Eph. 5:21).
Christ talked about wholeness of personality and a full life, not
the mediocre drag of a worm. He intended his followers to make
life itself their vocation while on this earth. Eternal life does not
begin in heaven, but here, in time, when the new birth takes
place.

Viktor Frankl, in *Man's Search for Meaning*, provides one
of the best illustrations that life is for living — at all times,
including the worst of times. He spent several years in a Nazi
concentration camp in which the prisoners were deprived of
their identity, all their possessions, as well as opportunities to
make any decisions, even small ones, like which potato to eat.

He found that those prisoners who no longer accepted responsibility for their present existence, but lived only in their
memories, soon died. Those who believed that even in that grim
situation life expected something of them, found strength to
survive. In that dismal camp, the prisoners had only one
freedom left to them and that was to choose their attitude toward those difficult circumstances. They could choose to be.
And when they chose to be, life gained significance for them.

Any object, or life itself, becomes meaningful if it is worth
something to someone. A Christian's life is worth a great deal
to God. Didn't God love the world so much he gave his son for
it? If he loves the individual that much, that person has much
reason to love him or herself. At least as much as the person

loves the neighbor. When a person gives this redeemed life over to God, God gives back to that person his or her true self to serve him. God doesn't return a shell or an empty husk of a body with the Holy Spirit rattling around inside. He gives to the believer his or her own personality sanctified by the Holy Spirit.

Christ living in me, not a worm. That is meaningful living.

The common-sense approach

6

Katie: *Wouldn't it make the most sense to forget about being employed by a church institution, like this college, and find a job in a secular business? At least then my money problems with four kids wouldn't be so tough.*

You: *Right. There'd be a lot less hassle and you could still serve the Lord at your job.*

Katie: *Sometimes I'm sure tempted to quit and go where the money is. I'm tired of counting pennies instead of dollars.*

You: *But once you've had your vision aroused by the Spirit of Christ, is it ever possible to be satisfied with anything else? Will money quiet that inner calling?*

The war years were crowding past me. I was about nineteen and my life had hit the doldrums despite the brisk movement of the war activities around me. One evening I wandered into the church basement for the youth meeting. The kids were down on their knees praying. At the moment I could think of nothing more boring and ridiculous. I wanted to turn and run.

However, the hunger in my own spirit prompted me to stay. The events over the next few months as a member of this youth group changed the direction of my life. Christ became more than an idea or even an ideal. He became a reality and the Christian life exciting.

Our youth group was not large, but we enjoyed a closeness with one another difficult to describe. We also had an urge to be open to God and what he had for us. His will was important. Bible study followed as a natural activity. My new Scofield Bible was thumbed and underlined as the meaning of passage after passage burst upon me.

We gathered every Tuesday evening and sometimes after church on Sundays for "fellowship." When the church council preempted our week-night spot, we felt chagrined by their lack of feeling for the spiritual interests of its youth. But then the congregation was not accustomed to energetic youth groups.

I recall our deep concern as young people for one another's spiritual welfare and also for the reputation of Christ. I have never since experienced the freedom with which we admonished one another if we thought something in the other person's life might hinder the honor of Christ. We did it without offense. Was it only the innocence of youth?

The criticism leveled against the Jesus people of the sixties, that they were simplistic and condescending to those who didn't have their truth, could have been aimed at us also. We were serious; we were simplistic in our faith, and probably condescending toward those who couldn't grasp our open, joyous approach to Christianity.

Sociologists may be able to explain youth groups like ours, which sprang up across the country at that time in terms of group dynamics. Young people away from home for the first time. War pressures. An unstable economy. Perhaps so. I also believe that whatever is of the Spirit will lead to Christ's glory.

For a short time while we were young together, we cultivated an awareness of the spiritual dimension of life until it became the most important part of our lives. It transcended the meagerness of life in a dingy "light-housekeeping" room with a two-burner coal-oil stove and window-ledge "refrigerator." It gave direction and purpose for life for that period, and for some of us, for a lifetime. I call it the "faith" approach.

In later years, the reality of rent money and tuition fees for classes and the awareness that prayer does not provide instant results hit me hard. But my experience as a new Christian gave me a permanent sense of direction and a willingness to be responsive to God's Word. I wanted to be known as a person of faith.

At times the faith-way has seemed diametrically opposed to common sense — almost fanatical, in fact. Yet I continue to believe that common sense belongs to the rationalists and the two — faith and common sense — stand in the relation of the natural and the spiritual.

Without being aware of it, though one may have supported the principles of faith for years, close examination reveals one to have joined the camp of the rationalists. At one time it made sense to love the Lord with all one's heart, to keep the Sabbath Day holy, to honor one's father and mother, to love one's neighbor, not to commit adultery or to covet, lie or steal, like the Pharisees. But with the passing years it seems to make more sense to find a path around these commandments and to make one's own experience and awareness of life the standard of behavior.

For such a person the answers to life lie within oneself. The teachings of Christ are accepted only if they fit one's lifestyle. God eventually becomes a mere abstraction, an impersonal force, rather than a living person.

I find a body of rationalization growing around the concept of the home and family. To the natural or common-sense person, it makes more sense to have trial marriages and to encourage divorce when a marriage falls apart than for both partners to accept at the outset that the grace of God will be sufficient for fifty years or more. People can't hold out that long, they tell me, forgetting that God can.

To the natural person, for a parent to accept full responsibility for their children when mother or father could be doing something more fulfilling seems folly. Children should never restrict either parent.

To the common-sense person to wait years on the backside of the desert taking care of aging parents, studying or working at menial tasks, is a waste of time.

To the common-sense person, the spiritual weapons of faith, truth and prayer are replaced by Roberts Rules of Order, constitutions, statistics and accounts of "how other churches grew successfully." Meetings are begun with the reading of Scripture and prayer, but thereafter biblical principles are not considered again during the session. Common sense prevails instead. Is there a problem? A committee is called into being to work it out, which is a more reasonable solution to the problem than finding out what scriptural principles might apply. What the group decides together is accepted as right even though the decision may not meet the test of Christ's teaching. It just makes better common sense.

To the common-sense person, society's standards of success are his or her standards. Self-sacrifice, cross-bearing, traveling the hard and narrow road, all yield to an insistence on security and moving at full speed down the superhighway with clear road signs. No congregation, committee or individual should be expected to function efficiently without the assurance that the Spirit will work predictably. To accept a task, any task, out of debtorship to God, and to yield to its disciplines at the price of personal discomfort seems ridiculous if it means bypassing personal financial and social success.

Common-sense people do not require their leaders to have spiritual power — only the ability to manage groups effectively and to speak in such a way that the congregation stays awake.

With a common-sense approach the agenda, the methodology, the goals, are all human. With the faith approach, they are Christ's and he is in control.

During the dark ages of the Israelites, the period of the judges, the country was overrun with common-sense people: "Every man did what was right in his own eyes." Political and moral corruption covered the land like a smog. The people had no room for self-giving, love and sacrifice. They hadn't learned that the person who loses his or her life for Christ's sake finds it.

The faith-approach to life comes from a vision of God. It puts his will first in all matters. It recognizes that all of life is grace. It asks at every turning in life, not what does life owe me, but what do I owe God? The life of faith doesn't just happen. Each believer makes it happen through choices.

A place to stand

7

Katie: *Well, we did it — finally finished that degree. Maybe now I can move into a lounge chair on the patio and watch the grass grow.*

You: *Well, why not?*

Katie: *The security of the moment feels terrific, but how long can I relax before I'll be moving backwards?*

Each day since the last snow I have watched the tulips and crocuses we planted last fall push their way through the ground. Before they sprouted, I wondered fleetingly if I had planted them too deep. Today green tips are emerging strong and healthy and are establishing their place in the sun.

The robins have returned to nest in one of our trees. A meadowlark broke the morning stillness with its cry of joy yesterday. Behind the house I hear the mourning dove calling all nature to sorrow with it. Before long the bustling sparrows will set up housekeeping again in the crosspiece of the clothesline. Each bird is also looking for a place for the summer.

As I watch summer gaining strength, I know I will miss the children's attempts at place-making again this year. How long has it been since they last hauled out blankets, tarps and clothespins to create a tent over the clothesline? Most of their energy was devoted to frantic pinning and stretching, very little to sitting in the airtight compartment which resulted.

Sweaty and tired, they sometimes relaxed briefly to munch crackers and drink Kool-aid in their "own place."

Now they, like other young people, are looking for a different kind of place of their own. College students are looking for a place to work for the summer, graduates for something more permanent. I see them examine anxiously the "Positions Open" ads tacked to the bulletin board at the college where I teach.

Keith Miller writes in *The Becomers* that everyone behaves as if he or she were on an uncharted, and often unconscious, search for a place of one's own. We have come to accept that in God's economy he has a place for each one. From the time we are children we begin this search for our place — a place of security, acceptance, identity and happiness. Young or old, we keep looking.

As a young girl I used to lie on the sunny side of the woodpile in the backyard, gazing to the blue skies decorated with free-floating clouds, wondering about the place I would have some day in life. The woodpile is long gone, but the desire for a place remains.

This longing for an emotional niche where we can be free to be ourselves, to love, and to risk failure is almost instinctive. To lose it means to stop growing and become stagnant. Yet somehow most of us believe that when we find this place up ahead where we will fit in, it will turn out to be a ledge, a stopping point on life's journey. It will be an arriving.

Miller points out that some people believe that their place is achieving certain material goals or a particular status on some achievement ladder. They look for a certain grade or degree, a particular person for a mate, a particular job, a better home, and so forth. In looking for their place, these people want some visible way to measure growth or achievement, something they can use to assure themselves they have arrived. Yet often when they get that degree, that job, that new house, it doesn't satisfy.

What then is a Christian's place? Certainly not a spot

where the person can settle down and watch the grass grow. A Christian's place is never a destination, like a higher position in the church hierarchy, more time spent successfully in Bible study and prayer, the ability to give more money to the church, or even more committee positions. The Christian's place is more like a journey, as it was for Abraham and Moses.

Whenever a Christian wants to stop and build a permanent stopping place, that particular situation will carry with it the opportunity to surrender securities, place one's trust more fully in God's hands, and through a leap of faith move on. Any time a Christian thinks he or she has arrived in the Christian life — has full understanding of how to love, forgive, pray, lead, teach, give — the way opens up to new awarenesses. Each place, as one arrives at it, leads only to another opportunity. Always the new place ahead involves risk and vulnerability. God gives security for a while, but only for a little while, to develop courage to move on.

Losing God
through nature

8

Katie: *Does getting close to nature necessarily mean getting closer to God?*

You: *For some it probably does.*

Katie: *Can't God be as close to us in a house as in a tent under a tree by the lake? Are God and nature the same?*

Because Americans do not deliberately whittle their gods and idols out of wood, stone or metal so as to see and handle them, they do not always recognize the gods they unknowingly worship — the god of nature, for example.

Most serious Christians do not leave God at home with forgotten lawn-mowing chores while on their annual two-week vacation. But some do think they will get closer to God as they get closer to nature, and that as they revel in natural beauties they are learning more about him. Some vacationers believe they can commune with God through nature and that nature can furnish them with the true knowledge of the Lord. Nature becomes the way God is revealed to them. And that doesn't hold true, says theologian Elizabeth Achtemeier in *The Feminine Crisis in the Christian Faith*. God can only be known through his Word and his acts in history, with the sending of his son, Jesus Christ, as the ultimate act. All over the nation, people are figuratively and literally "lifting their eyes unto the hills" in the mistaken certainty that through nature's wonders they will be granted knowledge of the Lord.

Yet I can't deny that as I enjoy the gentle quietness of the early morning sun rising over a mountain lake, or listen to the surf beat steadily against the shore, God seems very near, much nearer than behind a store counter or a kitchen sink. Doesn't that feeling count for something?

To relax with the wonders of nature and to humbly recognize that God is the creator of all is one thing. God has given us all things to enjoy. However, in our present society, with the trend toward the occult and the primitive, the bigger danger is to make God, the Lord over nature, into a nature god — to think of him as part of nature — which is a form of idolatry.

America is astir with a strong movement to return to nature, to grub in the soil with one's hands, to build one's own cabin, to wrest a living from the elements. The movement springs partly from a reaction to the complicated strenuous city life and the pressures of an impersonal computerized society, and partly from a desire to restore ecological balance. Those who are also religiously inclined are convinced they will also get closer to God as they get closer to the soil.

Achtemeier points out that such natural religion is never sufficient, for to turn God into a nature god is to become a Baal worshiper. These primitive worshipers rarely considered an image to contain their god or to be their god. The idol of stone, wood or metal was not god but a transparent symbol through which the god was revealed. Thus anything could be an image or idol for these people — stones, trees, groves, plain wooden poles. For these people the divine became known to humans through objects in the created world.

This is exactly the issue the second commandment speaks against, she says, when it states that people shall make no graven images. God was showing the Israelites that nothing in the created world was adequate to reveal him, including lakes, trees, flowers and mountains, even if found in the land where Jesus walked and talked. God makes himself known to humans only by his own acts and words.

While nature is assuredly beautiful, refreshing and relaxing and not to be despised, it does not show God's plan of redemption; it cannot reveal Christ's sacrifice, death and resurrection. Nature does not teach God's forgiveness or give assurance of eternal life. Nature cannot take the place of God and his Word.

One of the dangers of this subtle form of Baal worship is that it denies God's lordship over human beings and their responsibility to him, she continues. The god of nature makes few demands upon its worshipers. It is completely impersonal — simply a great life force, and therefore has no will of its own. It only asks that those who come to it get lost in it — lose their "identity and float in the bottomless abysses of beauty. Its aim is to merge our souls with the great soul of nature and thus to share in nature's supposedly divine life and truth and peace."

By contrast, Jehovah-God comes to us as a person. The God of the Bible is never an it or a one or a being. We are not lost in the crowd before this God. We are not a "nameless nonentity, blurred into nature's soul." And it is impossible to remain neutral before or to ignore our responsibility to him.

As we continue to enjoy and admire God's creation, let's not forget that between God and his creation is his revelation through his Word. Anything less is a return to idol worship.

Newspaper faith

9

You: *What do you think you trust more, the Bible or the newspaper about the way to live your life?*

Katie: *The Bible, of course.*

You: *Don't forget that the next time you get caught in a tight situation.*

As the light changed to green, I pressed my foot on the accelerator. The motor whined like a tired child, coughed once, and quit. I tried again. No success.

I was in a strange city. The night was icy cold, the hour late, and the streets empty of cars. I looked around, wondering what to do. A group of young men detached themselves from the wall under a street light and ambled toward me. Thoughts of kidnapping, rape, murder, robbery, flooded my mind for a second, and I gave the accelerator a vicious shove.

"Having trouble?" A cheerful face looked down at me.

I yielded the door to the smile. One tight-jeaned fellow crawled in beside me and did gentle things to the accelerator. Another lifted the hood and jiggled a few items. In about three minutes I could say thanks and be on my way.

Although such an incident could have ended otherwise, nothing out of the ordinary happened at that street corner. But my mind had been trapped by the fear created by newspaper articles which emphasize ordinary people are out to harm other ordinary people. I was exercising newspaper faith at that moment — not biblical faith. And I find I have lots of company.

If the story of the Good Samaritan had been written today, he probably would have ended up at the inn alone. Over a hot drink, I can hear him telling the other travelers about the guy with the busted head who wouldn't accept his help because he didn't recognize him or because he wasn't a card-carrying Mennonite, Methodist or Baptist from his hometown.

Newspaper faith is powerful. It can slowly, but surely, erode the faith of unwary Christians to the point of paralysis. **The writer of "Hebrews" describes the exploits of faith of early followers of God. They gave their lives for others, they spoke out against sin, they obeyed the call to follow God's leading into strange territory to take on new tasks. "Through faith they overthrew kingdoms, established justice, and saw God's promises fulfilled" (11:33 *NEB*).** Newspaper faith, on the other hand, convinces Christians that the powers of evil are in control and God's truth has been vanquished by changing the focus to stories which highlight "man's inhumanity to man."

Newspaper faith teaches that the world has only one important person in it — you. Take care of No. 1, make yourself happy by any and all means, and you're doing the best and wisest thing in the world. Stranded travelers, because of accident, poverty, race or other circumstances, are not your responsibility. Let the legislators take care of such problems.

Newspaper faith teaches through the advice of advertisers, syndicated columnists, movie producers and television programmers that happiness is the ultimate end of human life, and if it is not achieved immediately in a relationship or work situation, the best procedure is to throw the person who hinders your happiness out of the position, marriage or family — or relocate yourself in another state. Biblical faith teaches forgiving love, patient love, yielding love and provides power through the Spirit to live with less-than-perfect persons.

Newspaper faith teaches that "I'm OK, you're OK" — a needed understanding, but only if it is not accepted as the

whole truth. This phrase leaves out an important element —
us, or you and me together. Biblical faith teaches the sanctity
of the family and the glory of the community of believers. It
emphasizes the necessity and availability of resources within
these institutions to strengthen and enhance our lives together.

Newspaper faith teaches that you can change your personal quirks and weaknesses through the right combination of
reading best-sellers, attending seminars, undergoing analysis,
buying the right clothes and losing weight. You can achieve
perfection with the right amount of determination and disregard for others. Scripture teaches that the saving grace of God
can bring the human being and God into a right relationship
and break the power of sin.

Newspaper faith teaches that violent action and words can
solve problems on all levels (interpersonal, church community,
national and international) more quickly and surely than the
way of suffering love. Newspaper faith has many doctrinal
statements, although rarely are they found formulated into a
carefully documented confession of beliefs, for each person
picks and chooses according to personal preferences and convenience.

Can a Christian avoid being seduced by newspaper faith?
Yes, by answering the Old Testament command to the Is-
raelites: Choose you this day whom you will serve, the God of
Scripture or the spirit of the world.

What I
don't want
for Christmas

10

Katie: *At times I have this longing I can't handle for something more than tinsel and wrappings, trees and stars.*

You: *I have that longing too. I have it deep inside — I want to stand and worship the Christ in the beauty of holiness without the frippery and frappery — just Christ and me.*

Although it seems too early for anyone but eager children, harried housewives and Christian education directors to think seriously about Christmas, I would like to present what I call my Christmas non-gift list. These are the things I don't want for Christmas.

First, I don't want less commercialization at Christmas. I have come to see that buying and selling is a normal condition of our society. Jesus was born into a very commercial world. His ministry was performed in the midst of rank commercialism. He watched the temple abused by the money-changers. He ejected a legion of devils from the man of the Gadarenes and sent them into a herd of swine, fully aware that the village people were more concerned about their financial loss than the healing of the man. Jesus did not run away from commercialism or merely decry it.

I don't want less commercialization, but I do want the perceptivity to know when its power is controlling my life. I want the courage to resist the pressure to make card lists, gifts, food, clothes, parties and banquets more important than people and personal relationships. The latter was Christ's concern. May it be mine.

Second, I don't want the mystery of God demystified. I don't want God reduced to a simple mathematical equation so that I can feed the data about him into a giant computer to find out why he loves sinful humanity, how he works in a person's life to bring him or her to the knowledge of forgiveness, or even why a person's heart hungers to know him better.

I don't deny the longing which overcomes a person at times to reach out in the darkness and to feel that he is skin or to hear his voice audibly — to prove he is real by the senses. Yet to have the revelation of God completely analyzed and reduced to concrete terms would bring a meeting with him to the level of an encounter with the butcher.

Within humankind is a constant pressure to analyze and to systematize what we do not fully understand, so the great truths of the Bible are hammered into a three-point alliterative sermon or four simple spiritual laws. The events of God's relationship to humankind are cut up into dispensations; the experience of God's indwelling the believer becomes a diagram with circles and thrones and dots and arrows; and the end of the age and the Lord's return show up as a complicated chart with crisscrossing lines and arrows.

All of these may have their place at some time, yet to be able to systematize, to organize, to put into order, gives the individual a sense of power and control whether this concerns a shopping list or the revelation of God to humankind. To systematize is to be in control.

This Christmas I want to stand in awe and wonder with the shepherds and wise men at the glory of the incarnation. I want to experience with Isaiah "the Lord high and lifted up." To demystify God is to do away with faith and worship and make of his worshipers totally secular beings.

Third, I do not want things seen to become the evidence of things not seen. In Hebrews 11 the Apostle Paul tells us that

our faith-life is to be the evidence of the supernatural world —
the things we cannot see with the physical eye. By faith we are
to believe in Christ, in sins forgiven, in life after death, in
Christ's return, in his power to work through us.

I do not want jeweled crosses or lapel pins, badges and
buttons, mottoes and posters, Jesus watches and bumper-
stickers, certificates, emblems and constitutions to become the
evidence of the Christ-life. Instead, this Christmas, I pray that
the cup of cold water for a thirsty person, the walking of a
second mile with a weary individual, the gift of a coat may be
more clearly the "evidence of things not seen."

Last, this Christmas I do not want an end to questioning. I
realize that often a person's faith is judged valid to the extent he
or she accepts all ecclesiastical pronouncements without em-
barrassing questions. The person who makes others uncomfortable by probing is labeled unspiritual and out of place. I
believe we need more questioning about the church's responsibility regarding the social issues of our time. We need more
questioning about what is happening to the family and the
unity of the church. We need questions and a readiness to
follow the leading of the Spirit in the answers.

Here ends my non-list.

*. . . about
the human
condition*

The search
for greatness

11

Katie: *I caught a glimpse of a truly great person today.*
You: *Did she fly in from Washington or Hollywood?*
Katie: *No, she lives in this town. She's old and not well off,
and probably few people really know her. I heard her ask
someone to forgive her callousness in having neglected her
responsibility to a discouraged friend.*

Before you begin reading, stop for a minute to list the
names of ten people you consider to be truly great men and
women of God. Keep in mind you are listing "great" people, not
merely "important" ones. Too hard? Then try for five.

To pinpoint the great among us these days is sometimes
difficult because we have misplaced or entirely lost what
greatness is. Does it mean someone frequently in the headlines?
Or perhaps someone who heads up a big institution? Or
someone who has made it to the top in athletics, movies or
television? Or someone who is an accomplished singer or
speaker?

For centuries the history of humankind has included the
record of great persons, or heroes, whose stories were told to
encourage and inspire the young. These heroes of history and
fiction were persons of courage, honor and integrity who were
willing to sacrifice themselves on behalf of truth and righteousness. Yet today all these terms I have just used are slipping

from our vocabulary and the concepts behind them as well. Honor? Who concerns him or herself about honor anymore? What about sacrifice? A concept almost as rare as the passenger pigeon. And integrity is for clods who don't want to get ahead.

As a society we have lost our true heroes and gained two other kinds of "greats" — the celebrity and the anti-hero. And unfortunately, what happens in society at large soon drifts over into church life.

A celebrity is simply a person with high visibility, often because he or she has a good p.r. person somewhere in the background. People are celebrities not necessarily because they are great, but because they have achieved in some nationally accepted activity like athletics, or the mass media.

The church readily accepts national celebrities as heroes of the faith; sometimes it's hard to tell them apart. Both bounce jauntily to the platform — it would never do to have the congregation or audience believe they didn't eat their Crunchies for breakfast — flash a toothy smile, and then belt it out. The symbol of the modern celebrity is a microphone in one hand.

I'll admit to disappointment when I find large religious gatherings splattered with celebrities. The message I get is that the best models for Christian living are athletes and folk and rock singers. Each of these has his or her place, but it seems to me a deliberate attempt to have the young identify with our culture instead of with Christ and what he stands for in any calling.

But another kind of hero substitute is becoming more popular — the "lovable bum" as literary critic Edmund Fuller describes him in *Man in Modern Fiction*. These anti-heroes may be "shiftless, drunks, amoral, wards of society, yet if you don't love them, you are a self-righteous bigot, hard of heart by contrast to the author's compassion and love for the common clay of humanity."

I see Archie Bunker of *All in the Family* television fame as one of these hero substitutes whom America has warmly welcomed in her arms. Archie, the lovable bigot — not bigoted enough so that we hate him violently, but just bigoted enough that we can laugh at his antics and forget that his kind, stepped up a few notches, was responsible for Auschwitz, for lynchings in the U.S. up until the 1930s, for terrorism by the Ku Klux Klan, and for ghettoes and racial riots. But Archie makes an enjoyable hero. He does and says a few stupid things, but he is really a likeable chap.

Fuller states that in the anti-hero of our modern fiction we have the denial that men and women are what their consistent, voluntary (and involuntary) patterns of action make them. He cites the example of one heroine, 18 years old, addicted to drugs, sexually delinquent, mother of an illegitimate child, who moves to prostitution. She says at one point in the novel rather reproachfully, "You think I'm a tramp." And the reader is expected to respond, "Shucks, kid, just going around doing what every tramp does doesn't make a good, sweet, clean little kid like you a tramp."

What you do doesn't determine what you are is the refrain of today's society. You are a beautiful person as long as you are an accepting person of anything and everything and have an enormous capacity to overlook. The ugly people are the ones who narrowly insist that maybe God has a few standards and values that make life worthwhile.

Noting the tremendous popularity of *The Godfather*, both book and movie, I continue to wonder how twisted our society has become. The story is about the patriarch of a Mafia family who rules his family kingdom by violence. He murders like I squash a mosquito. His way of life, including the fact that he brings his own son into his pattern of behavior, is deemed virtuous and great by the general public. As Fuller says, the anti-hero thinking inverts what is generally considered "bad" into a curious kind of good, to which the normal life stands as a kind of bad.

True greatness — where does it lie? Not in high visibility, not in attaining top positions, not in having many talents, not in amassing and using brute strength — but in achieving the mind of Christ. "Let this mind be in you which was also in Christ Jesus: who . . . made himself of no reputation and took upon him the form of a servant" (Phil. 2:5, 6, 7).

Now make out your list of ten great men and women of God. You'll find them all around you.

Littered people

12

Katie: *If that guy'd wash his hair a little more often and use more deodorant, more people would love him.*

You: *But God loves him with or without deodorant. It's just we people who can't stand him the way he is.*

Katie: *Yeah, but God is God, and I'm a human being with a nose and eyes.*

This morning as I drove along the highway I noticed yesterday's droppings of cans and paper littering the ditch. An empty paper cup raced along the road before me until I caught up with it and the tires of the car ended its escapade.

Littering is illegal, but it still happens. When the trash level in the car gets too high, what can one do? Chuck it, of course, when no one is looking, according to litterers.

Littering isn't confined only to glass, paper, metal and plastic. We also litter people. According to Ken Reuter, we "batter them, dent them and rain on them until they rust and fall apart in our minds." He suggests if we look into the landscape of our mind, we will find a junkyard of persons we've discarded because they failed to come up to our unreal standards of perfection.

Our age of planned obsolescence has incorporated into us the same attitude toward people that we have toward things: Get rid of what you don't like. If a person doesn't match the decor of your thinking, get rid of him or her. Don't bother with persons who don't meet your standards of appearance or social status. Relay to a gossipy neighbor your disgust about the person who forgets to bathe, or who uses mediciny-smell mouthwash, or forgets to wash his or her greasy hair, and you have gotten rid of the individual. Discard the one who prefers Lawrence Welk to your classical records with one sweeping comment about boors. Add to this group the ones who forget to color coordinate their wardrobe or who talk without brakes. Throw all such people out of the window of your mind to be run over by the next traveler. They're not your kind.

Littered people come in other categories as well. The biggest category is "they." "They" represents the most powerful bloc of people on earth and most despised, for "they" control nearly everything we do, from the prices we pay for gas and food to how often we mow the lawn or go to church. "What will they think?" decides many issues, yet if every speaker substituted a name for every "they" when speaking, a lot of people would have to be dug out of the garbage heap.

Another big category of easily littered persons is bosses, especially the ones who can't make up their minds, or who make it up too fast, or who think they made it up and told you so, but then wibble-wobble all day long. This kind gets tossed into the trash barrel at coffee breaks often. But employees land there also — especially the kind who were born a *Schlepp*.

Another group of people who are quickly added and tossed aside are those who don't fit into the landscape of congregational life — the ones with bent opinions and open mouths. We easily litter them because it seems sure that God couldn't possibly work through such warped individuals.

At present another group of people get chucked out without a hearing, though many Christians may never have seen or talked to one. I refer to homosexuals. Most Christians would give a hardened murderer at least a chance to hear the gospel, but feel uncomfortable if a professed homosexual came to church. Yet by littering them, we deny them the opportunity to come close to God. We're convinced they're not redeemable.

Sometimes we litter even ourselves when we don't believe we are the kind of material God could use for his service. What could God do with an ordinary person without special talents in teaching, preaching or music? The Apostle Paul never thought less of himself than Christ thought of him. Though some people thought he was a little odd-looking and timid in his personal appearance, lacking celebrity appeal, he saw himself too precious to be littered. He boldly affirmed himself several times: "Follow my example as I follow Christ's" he told the Corinthians, Philippians and Thessalonians (1 Cor. 4:16; 11:1: Phil. 3:17; 1 Thess. 1:6).

Trash and people should never be in the same category. God doesn't want anyone to be littered, but all to come to full maturity in Christ Jesus. He is in the process of recycling, taking anyone who comes to him, marred, bent, scratched, even a bit rusty, and he says, "This person can be made new in Christ Jesus" (2 Cor. 5:17). To believe rebirth is possible is the beginning of church life and growth. Without believing that people can change by the power of the Spirit, there can be no church, no body of Christ — only a human organization with laws about littering.

The land
of forgiveness

13

You: *When did you last say "I'm sorry" to someone?*

Katie: *Who, me? No one says that anymore. That's old-fashioned. You just smooth the rough spot over or look for some way of getting rid of the guilt. It's okay to be yourself these days.*

You: *If there is no forgiveness to wash the dirt away, how do people ever return to real caring again?*

At six-thirty, as I was washing the dishes, my son came in from a short bike ride to tell me that if I wanted a seat at the service I was planning to attend that evening, I'd better hurry. People were piling into the auditorium by the hundreds.

These early birds were probably mistaken about the time, I surmised. The meeting didn't start until eight. At seven-thirty when I entered the large auditorium, it was nearly full, and the people were continuing to stream in. Children. Young people. Middle-aged. Oldsters. Some with tape recorders, others with cameras and notebooks.

The bleachers behind the speaker's podium filled up as well as every seat on the main floor. Latecomers squatted on the floor or dangled their feet from the stage.

And then 81-year-old Corrie ten Boom walked in. A standing ovation greeted her dignified entrance. Her story has become world famous, first through *The Hiding Place* by John and Elizabeth Sherrill, and since then by her personal appearances and additional writings.

Her family's commitment to hide Jews in their home in Holland from Hitler's army resulted in their internment in the dreaded concentration camps. Corrie's father and sister died there; she survived the atrocities.

As the service began, the question uppermost in my mind was why so many people had come. Few speakers draw such a crowd in little Hillsboro, a community of about 3,000 residents. Had they come for the same reason they watch a horror movie? Did they hope to be titillated by her accounts of life in a concentration camp?

Corrie ten Boom's lively sense of humor immediately won her a place with her audience. Her deep-rooted humility was also apparent. "Some people think I have a great faith," she said. "Instead I have faith in a great God."

But even these admirable attributes are not enough to pull so many people from television sets and football games to wait an hour and a half. If they had come to hear shocking stories about Nazi cruelty, they were bound to be disappointed. She mentioned only a few of her own experiences briefly.

How can one then account for her charisma?

I think the appeal was her simple message of strength for daily life by the Spirit of Christ for people in which the life of faith has all but been edged out by individualism, professionalism and the democratic process. She brought the same message which saints of another age have preached. She reminded me of Hannah Whitall Smith, F. B. Meyer, Watchman Nee and Andrew Murray. All have proclaimed that the victorious life is possible in any circumstance.

Corrie ten Boom moved away from the world of lists, figures, budgets and programs. Her message was made effective because she could say, "An abundant life is possible for you. God is sufficient for any trial. My life proves it." She answered the longing for a deeper sense of wholeness with God, with humanity, and within oneself. She spoke to the chronic ache in the heart which never appears on a standard church agenda, an agenda concerned with the purchase of new choir robes, lists of names for devotionals and babysitting chores.

In *The Hiding Place* she writes of the time she stood naked together with hundreds of other women prisoners while the guards gawked and laughed; of the time she waited many long hours in the icy-cold dawn for roll call, her feet grotesquely swollen; of the time she saw her sister physically abused by the guards; of the time she lived in a room so filthy with fleas and lice the guards would not enter; of the time her only bed was vomit-covered straw; of the time the news of her father's death reached her. After each incident she could say, "At the moment I needed the strength to love and forgive, God gave it to me."

I thought I heard her saying at this meeting: There is a land of forgiveness and love. Each one of you can dwell in it. But this territory is in the human heart and is inhabited only through trust in God. You can live in it regardless of health, family problems, financial difficulties, loss of purpose. If God could help me in prison, he can help you here in America.

*   *   *

Several years ago I agreed, once again, to accept a cat as a house pet. He was part Siamese, black, and strikingly beautiful. But he refused to act like a pet.

He deigned to pet us if we accepted his terms. He dominated the household with a loud, demanding voice. My interpersonal relationships with Gabriel, as he was named because of his lack of resemblance to the archangel, were poor — very poor. In fact, the situation deteriorated daily. He wasn't okay, and I wasn't okay. We thought bad thoughts about each other, even though I was the one who made sure he was fed, watered and let in and out of the house on demand.

Finally, Daughter No. 3, sensing the situation was explosive, became my advocate, and found Gabriel a new home on a farm where his demand for total freedom had fewer ill consequences.

If that unloved cat (on my part — not the children's) had been a spouse, a child, a fellow worker, or a friend, would I have followed the same procedure and agreed to get rid of the person? How does one adjust to a disappointing relationship with another person, other than to call it quits? How does one adjust to a frustrating marriage? And who hasn't had a marriage with its frustrating moments — or even days and weeks? Should one be expected to adjust or is it okay to quit relating?

The answer depends on what values one cherishes. If personal happiness is top priority, then obviously the only solution is to part. If other values are more important, there must be other answers.

My daughter saw separating cat and mother as the best solution. Few would disagree with her — it was only a cat. But when it comes to human relationships the answer isn't so simple. Few people are limitless in their power to expand their personalities to move in and out of relationships without being hurt — or hardened. Human beings are limited in their power to redeem and make perfect what the imperfect self has messed up.

I agree with one marriage counselor that the answer to problems in personal relationships is basically a religious one. How can persons who are very different in gender and temperament live together harmoniously? Does behavioral science have the answers? Can life together become more beautiful if society forgets such values as lifetime faithfulness, self-giving and responsibility to family, friends and community?

Paul Popenoe writes that Christians claim there is a power they can draw upon that can root out the deeply embedded selfishness and set them free to love redemptively and live at peace with others. But they don't demonstrate this claim when confronted by tough situations.

Now, as I think about that cat, I know I could have learned to live with it — if I had wanted to. But I didn't want to. I didn't want that cat disturbing my sleep. Which is probably the reason personal relationships fall apart. The effort to love is too great, although the values involved are worth it. To separate is easier.

The glory
has not departed

14

You: *How old are you?*

Katie: *Hitting fifty.*

You: *How do you feel about being that old?*

Katie: *Great, simply great. It's great to be middle-aged.*

You: *You're kidding. No one likes to be middle-aged, because it means you'll soon be old and a back number and no one will want you around.*

Katie: *I think every age in life can have its splendors, if we let it.*

You: *Well, go ahead and see what happens. You'll soon feel just as old as the other middle-agers.*

Something has happened. I think the pedestal on which youth was enshrined has toppled over. The young among us have been tumbled onto common ground and forced to shift with the rest of us. When the pedestal is raised again, it may possibly have adults on it.

During the fifties and sixties, our society openly worshiped the young. Youth was the age to be. Advertising was directed to their tastes, desires and fancies. Grownups mimicked their clothes, their language and actions. Education was a service geared mostly to the needs of the young. Even Christian education was mainly a youth movement; and youth activities

were a high priority in the church, for weren't youth the leaders
of tomorrow?

Well, that tomorrow has arrived, and the leaders haven't
shown up despite all the coddling. The widespread dearth of
leadership is an agreed-upon fact. The emphasis is shifting
away from the young to a new group. People are proclaiming
"it's great to be an adult." And why can't adults be the leaders
of today as well as tomorrow?

In *The Mature Mind*, first published in 1949, Harry
Overstreet writes that society glamorized youth because adulthood presented no inspiring image to either group. Youth
looked at the adults around them falling into a dreary proces-
sion of years filled with routine and boredom. Adulthood had no
intrinsic dignity and worth. No challenge. Overstreet quotes
William Sheldon as saying the image of adulthood was "smug,
vulgar and deadening."

Youth resisted growing up because the only alternative to
being young was the physical state of adulthood. Maturity was
not a valid option. Adulthood was not seen as a time of
increasing power and fulfillment, only as a letting go, a making
the best of a boresome bargain. After the free joyous years of
youth were finished, you endured life.

During this period J. D. Salinger wrote the best seller *The
Catcher in the Rye*. Young people bought several million copies
and devoured its contents. Adults found the book dull. In it,
17-year-old Holden Caulfield, a high school flunkout, takes a
close look at the adults in his life — teachers, parents, administrators, friends — and rejects them all as phonies. His life's
ambition is to find some way of keeping children from "falling
over the cliff" into adulthood. He wants them to remain
perennially young.

At one point he wonders what will happen to all the girls he
knows. He deplores that they will probably marry "dopey
guys" who always talk about how many miles they get to a
gallon in their cars, guys that get sore and childish if you beat
them at golf or ping pong, guys that never read books, guys

that are boring. This image of the adult male disgusts him.

Though Holden's view of adulthood may not be entirely accurate, this unenticing portrait of grownup living spawned the generation gap and the resulting hippie movement and student riots of the late sixties. All singled out a weakness in adult life. It did not inspire.

Now the pendulum is changing. A new image of adulthood is emerging, which is creative and fulfilling. Society has raised its expectations of the older person. No more fumbling for rocking chair and slippers. The new challenge is to become a lifelong learner.

I am thrilled to see the many college advertisements inviting adults to join continuing education programs that do more than avoid boredom through crafts and hobbies. Adults are being encouraged to enroll in courses that stimulate the mind.

I sense also that more adults are accepting the fact that God can invade their lives and set them on a meaningful new course of discipleship. The adventure of Christian growth can be theirs. Youth have no monopoly here. Some adults are weary of the tenderfoot treatment they have received for decades in adult Sunday school classes. They yearn for more meat and fewer "nice times." As a result some are looking for opportunities for more intensive Bible study. Definitely a good sign.

Society is also changing its attitude toward retirement. Though much still needs to be done in this area, the term "retirement" is no longer wholly negative, denoting a period of uselessness before death comes. One sociologist suggests the term should be abolished and replaced by "lifestyle change." Certainly, retirement for many adults creates opportunities for church service at home and abroad.

Adulthood need not be a glory departed. Youth has its great moments to cherish, but adulthood has even more to offer — but only if you join the group who have made growth their priority. If you plan to do any joining in the next months, join the adults who are celebrating their adulthood.

Consider
the dandelions

15

Katie: *Get out there and start working on that mass of
yellow.*
You: *Why?*
Katie: *The neighbors will talk. You know it.*
You: *Let 'em talk, I like dandelions.*

Spring rains and warm sunshine added to store-bought
fertilizer gave us a bumper crop of dandelions in the backyard.
If Jesus had walked the plains of Kansas instead of the Holy
Land, I'm sure he would've said, "Consider the dandelions;
they toil not neither do they spin."

The children brought in a fistful of flowers and we admired
their vague beauty together. I read years ago that the true
mother enshrines all floral offerings from her children in a vase
on the living room table, or at least in a milk carton on the
refrigerator. I think those dandelions soon went down the
disposal. At the moment I was too conscious of the energy it
would take to eradicate them.

Like a true Middle American, I've been out in the backyard
digging dandelions. I've been thinking long thoughts as I cut
them short; I'm not sure how Middle American that is.

If a person catches the roots just right with the cutting
tool, the dandelions break off with a quiet squirch. Then one can
move onto the next. And the next. There are always more.

Some attitudes in life multiply like dandelions. Criticism is one. How ridiculously easy to push or be pushed into harsh criticism. Just make one untidy remark about the person next door, and you've got a following.

I wish it were as easy to get people to laugh at themselves. I read a good many religious periodicals, and I must admit that we Mennonites are a straitlaced bunch. When the history books are written, we won't be remembered for our ability to laugh at our individual or collective foibles. The Jews get an A-rating at this. The divine right of Mennonites doesn't make room for much humor.

Out there stabbing the plants, I asked myself why I didn't just forget the persistent weeds. The answer: I'm afraid of what "they" — that nebulous authority which wields tremendous authority — will say. What would they think of my gold-frosted half-acre?

The power of "they" is Herculean. "They" decide whether we go to church or stay at home, what we wear and how much, whether we give and to whom, how much we pray and when, with whom we visit and why, what kind of car we drive or hide in the garage. We fear the "theys" most when our children turn up with a beard, outlandish clothes or friends, or take part in a protest demonstration. We fear what "they" will say more than what may be happening in our child's life. One dean of women of a large university said that mothers she talked with were often more concerned about their loss of respectability when their daughters got into difficulty than they were about the daughter.

Still stabbing the thickly leaved plants, I concluded that because we fear judgment by others, we mete out the same judgment. We become the "they" in the other person's life. The thought was not comforting. I almost wished I hadn't thought of it.

But then I had a better thought. Christ offered his followers soul freedom — the strength to move out from under the tyranny of "they" through the power of the Spirit. He knew that when his children are dominated by "they," their living space becomes confining, their outlook on life narrow, and their attitudes brittle and unyielding. "If the Son shall make you free, you shall be free indeed." He wants us to get our cues from him, not from the "theys" in our life.

Because Christ also taught the stewardship of influence, I sense that some young people are asking how much one should consider the feelings of others before adopting a course of action. How much should "What will people say?" affect one's behavior? We are experiencing an erosion of confidence in institutions such as government, schools and even the church and family. As the confidence gap grows, people become bolder to disregard the feelings of others, especially if "they" represents an institution rather than a person. At such times, even humor doesn't help to cement relations. Then it requires the biblical pattern of an honest admission of failure.

Before I returned to the house, I looked at the results of my afternoon's work. Some dandelions were already wilting in the daylight saving sun. Castaway, useless. The Apostle Paul wrote something about not wanting to be a castaway at the end of his life, so he was disciplining himself to stay in the running. Nowadays it's not always clear who has moved to the sidelines and who is still in the running. A session with the dandelions made it clear to me that when the church moves out of its present doldrums, I want to be ready to run with it.

Teach
me to dance

16

Katie: *Everyone at the service was clapping hands and moving about — but only from the shoulders up. I couldn't do it.*

You: *Why not? Was your arthritis getting the better of you?*

Katie: *No, my conditioning — I feel like a fool bouncing around.*

I have a book on my shelf which makes me uncomfortable. Its title is *Ask Me to Dance*. Hardly appropriate reading for a conservative, middle-aged matron occasionally bothered by corns.

But then when our minister suggested recently that we in the church have forgotten how to dance, I pulled Bruce Larson's book down from the shelf and found that foot troubles don't matter. You can dance with a broken leg.

The sermon had been on the Prodigal Son. The story is familiar. The son returns from the far country. The father meets him, embraces and kisses him, places a ring on his finger and shoes on his feet, and orders a festival. The grain-fed calf, reserved for special company, is killed, and the celebration begins with singing and dancing, for "My son was dead and is alive."

The older son returns from the fields. He hears the festive sounds of music and dancing (which some commentators believe was not actually dancing, but a form of dramatic choral singing in which the younger son's story was acted out). The older son refuses to enter the house, to which the father replies that everything he owns has belonged to the son these many years. Their relationship should have been a continual celebration. But the older son had never learned to enjoy it with freedom and abandonment. He had never learned to dance.

Larson writes that people today are asking the church to teach them to dance. People yearn to know how to be free and real about the right things. They want to know how to bless others. "Like Lazarus who came forth from the tomb filled with life but bound by grave clothes, they are unable to leap or sing," to experience exhilaration and freedom. They are still so bound, so determined to be nice, they have never learned to be real persons. They don't know how to celebrate.

I've thought about that father a lot. Why was it necessary to hold a big celebration? Weren't the hug and the kiss, the shoes and the robe, enough? Why the feasting and the singing? Why should we celebrate important events and days like births, marriages, Christmas, promotions and the smaller events like the first steps of a child, a homecoming, a new job, a reconciliation? Why make a big deal out of little things?

Why? Because in ritual and celebration we remember and transmit values. We keep alive and visible that which is most important. One father told me he wished the church had some specific rituals such as the Jews observe which feature the child asking, "What is the meaning of this rite? Why do we have communion? Why do we have (or not have) the washing of feet? Why do we have this particular way of conducting a wedding or a funeral?"

At a special event, our goal should be to emphasize in celebration the important truths of the Christian life. But sometimes these rituals and celebrations which have carried our values for years dry up — and then like the elder brother, we must learn to dance again.

Larson refers to the "solid, faithful, gray people" who never do anything very wrong, but who have never experienced the grace of Christ to live vibrantly. They exist. They endure. They survive. But life is not abundant. It is routine and work — and eventually bitterness and envy when they hear others celebrating life with Christ and don't know how to join in. And strangely, this celebrating is not done best by those who know the most about God theologically, but by those who are closest to the growing edge — the place of obedience.

Edna Wong was one who needed to learn to dance again. In *Turn Over Any Stone*, she writes of her long and painful struggle to find the answer to the problem of suffering. Her daughter gave birth to a retarded child. She couldn't accept "this garbled and diminished child as if a worker at the assembly belt in the womb factory fell asleep momentarily and blundered." Her spiritual recovery is long and difficult, but she returns to her family with the words, "I will sing to her. Do you know what I shall sing? 'Praise him, praise him, All ye little children; God is love, God is love.'" Her subconscious tells her that to sing is useless — the child cannot hear. Yet she sings jubilantly to silence the voices of doubt. At last these tormenters are completely routed by praise. This truth is a joyful discovery to her.

I think the father celebrated the son's homecoming with music and dancing to silence forever any doubts the young man might have he was not fully forgiven.

Yet how does one celebrate? Some say, "Go out for a steak!" "Buy a new dress!" "Bake a cake and have a party!" Others need parades, bands, firecrackers, liquor and food.

Real celebration needs no money. It begins with a truth, a value one wishes to uplift. Though you may not have touched each other as family members for a long time, this evening celebrate the family as a gift of God. Put your arms around one another and sing with Edna Wong, "Praise him, praise him, all ye little children; God is love, God is love." Then sing it again loudly, until you know it is real for you. Celebrate the family — the bridge of God between the individual and the world beyond — and keep celebrating until the elder son can't resist your joy and joins in.

Work, worship and leisure

17

Katie: *Three months of free time ahead. How are you going to use it?*

You: *Free time? You know you've already budgeted these months to within seconds.*

Katie: *Well, then, what are you exchanging time for these days?*

"Who are you?" How often that question is asked. I answer with my name and what I do for a living. "I am a teacher and writer," I say. Most people identify themselves in terms of what they spend most of their time at, and usually this is their job. A person's vocation has generally been considered the most significant part of life — a calling from God — which gives meaning to life as well as provides the cornflakes and milk for breakfast.

Some sociologists are suggesting that some strange things are happening to our traditional attitudes regarding work. With the rapid progress of technology, not everyone works at a job which adds immeasurably to the quality of life. Working on an assembly line, punching a keyboard, teaching kindergartners, may not be the kind of work which inspire long letters home. Not all persons want to be identified by their work, because it doesn't mean much to them.

Also, the number of hours a person works each week is

shrinking with each decade. In the post-Civil War period the average workweek was about 70 hours, or a 12-hour day, six-day week. This was reduced to a 60-hour week at the turn of the century, and further reduced to 50 hours before the Depression. Since 1900 there has been a reduction of several hours each decade. Recently a furniture factory in a neighboring community switched to a four-day week with about 39 hours of work.

So when you spend less and less time at your job, what do you write home about or talk about to friends? What then becomes the center of life? Obviously it's what you do when you aren't working — your leisure-time activities.

In my own small community, which in the basketball season fields a team for every age group from junior high through college, attending organized sports activities is a meaningful activity which provides grounds for existence night after night and provides something to talk about day after day.

Leisure time activities are moving into the center of life, writes Robert Lee in *Religion and Leisure in America*, and threaten to replace work as the basis of culture. America is becoming leisure-oriented rather than work-oriented.

Several decades ago many American housewives were encouraged to hope that when they had a fully automated kitchen and laundry, they would have free time on their hands. No such luck. Housewives are as busy, if not busier, than when they washed clothes on a scrubboard. Better equipment simply means more laundry is washed, more dishes are used, more cleaning attempted.

The prime reason people have less true free time is probably that with our increasing technology, our economy has shifted from a producer- or work-oriented society to a consumer-oriented one. Spending money and using goods is as important and takes as much time as earning the money. Most consumer goods, with built-in obsolescence, require much time for upkeep. A horse and buggy and the cistern required a certain amount of upkeep, but a car, plumbing and a lawn gobble up time.

One of the goals of many Americans is to own leisure-time goods because they provide meaning for living. Yet the more such goods a person acquires, the more time and energy are committed to using them. In our area, which boasts a large recreational reservoir with excellent boating and fishing facili- ties, families who own a boat and other related equipment want to get their money's worth out of them each season. They feel obligated to use them. But as a result, they will have less free time for other activities.

Longshoreman-philosopher Eric Hoffer makes the point that greater leisure such as we are experiencing should produce greater creativity. In the church, we should expect more free time would mean more people visiting the sick, helping the poor, and so forth. But it doesn't work out that way.

Our society is simply moving faster in the direction of materialistic pursuits, convinced that leisure is time that the individual owns personally and that the best leisure activity must be bought with money. What gets lost in the exchange are the fine arts, religion and family life. The issue is not the material goods owned and used, but that these are substituted for spiritual and social values.

Both leisure and work should give meaning to life because both involve time, a slice of eternity. How can the church encourage goals and values in a society in which work isn't the main part of life? How can the church help families find signifi- cant worship and fellowship experiences in ways other than a church family camp? How can the church use leisure to strengthen its purposes as it once used work? By using leisure time to work on these problems.

What shall we do about the devil?

18

Katie: *I don't like talking about the devil — too scary.*

You: *I agree. I can believe in evil, even in evil systems and structures, but not in a personal devil. That's taking Scripture a little too far.*

Katie: *You can't accept a personal devil? Lots of people who aren't Christians believe in him.*

In the late 1940s, a group of us college students visited in the warm kitchen of one of the older students on a cold, wintry night. As we sat around the kitchen stove and drank hot cocoa, the late evening conversation drifted to tales of the supernatural which soon matched Edgar Allen Poe's stories of mystery and horror.

Our host, who had lived in Russia in his youth, told us about a group of young men in one of the villages in the Crimea who had pledged themselves to worship the devil. One even agreed to sell his soul to humankind's ancient enemy and to seal the pact with his blood. After the agreement was made and the devil claimed possession of the man's body, he was endowed with superhuman strength — four or five strong men of the village could not restrain him. He literally climbed the wall in his frenzy.

The story was a good thriller, but a bad way to end an evening. I don't know whether we believed it, but my roommate and I dashed home down the deserted streets, looking neither to the right nor to the left.

Our attitude was not unusual. Christians frequently take one of two extremes when it comes to the devil. A few are so devil-conscious they push God to the periphery of their awareness and concentrate their main energies on fighting the devil. He is everywhere. All new ideas and activities are suspect. Such people usually manage to locate an evil spirit as the root of everything that doesn't fit their thinking. Such a view of life is highly contagious and can affect an entire congregation. They and their followers manage to stay in motion only by frantically calling on God to rebuke the devil at each weary step.

Fearful they may become extremists like these devil-routers, other Christians either ignore the devil entirely or joke about the red man with the ferocious features and leering eyes, long tail and three-pronged fork.

A strong belief in a personal devil who goes about as a "roaring lion seeking whom he may devour" is rare and as vague as a distant street sign in a dense fog. Instead, environmental factors, heredity and corrupt systems in government and institutions are to blame for evil today. Sin is a non-factor in life issues.

Though some Christians have an unbalanced view of the devil — either giving him too much room in their lives or not enough — the world seems to be growing in its open acknowledgment that he is alive and active. A fascination with magic, devil worship, spiritism, black masses and fortune-telling has swept the country. For some, this new movement is merely a fad and exciting new entertainment. For others, it is the opportunity to express their religious feelings in a more satisfactory way than worshiping God.

Because of the growing interest in the occult, we are seeing more novels, movies and television programs dealing with the subject. One of the first, *The Exorcist*, by William Peter Blatty, graphically portrays demon possession of a young girl in this era.

I began the book with some apprehension, for many best-sellers require too much slogging through verbal garbage to get at anything of value. This is also an ugly book with much foul language and obscene acts, as only a story about a powerful devil can be.

After members of the medical profession and a psychiatrist fail to heal the girl, a Roman Catholic priest is called in by the mother to exorcise the demon, even as parents asked Jesus to heal their demon-possessed children in his day. The girl recovers although the priest suffers a heart attack and dies as he battles the demon.

The question: Could demon possession take place today as it did in Christ's day? Reviews of this novel suggest most readers will regard it only as a skillfully written book with religious overtones — a good shocker or science fiction of another type — but certainly not something which could happen today.

As a novel it proves nothing, but it does reflect something of the spirit of our age. At the end of the story, another priest asks the mother of the demon-possessed girl if she has become a believer in God through her experience of exorcism. She replies she hasn't. "As far as God goes, I am a nonbeliever. But when it comes to a devil — well, that's something else . . . the devil keeps advertising, Father. The devil does lots of commercials."

All the evil in her world adds up to a devil, but, according to her, God never talks. She believes in the Father of evil, but not in God, for she sees more evidence of the former's power and work than of the latter's. She accepts that humankind has an enemy — but not a Redeemer-God.

How unlike Christians who think they are fighting the good fight of faith, but who have never discovered their enemy. Sin, Satan, evil powers, do not exist for them. I maintain the secular world, in its growing preoccupation with the occult, will discover the devil long before the church does, but for a different reason. They seek him to give him their allegiance. Christians deny his existence because to acknowledge it would mean joining the battle against him.

Children of Cain

19

Katie: *Whenever I hear a crowd yelling "Kill the referee" at the basketball game, I get upset.*

You: *Why? It doesn't mean a thing — just words.*

Katie: *But it does mean something. It says something about an attitude. If I told my children "I'll kill you" when I get upset with them, would they think of them only as words?*

The movie *Jaws* became one of the big money-makers in the entertainment world — with millions of dollars pouring in in America alone. *Jaws* is the story of a summer resort terrorized by a great white shark which stealthily swallows the swimmers. It is advertised as the "art of horror at its best," surpassing the violence of *The Godfather* and the grim evil of *The Exorcist* or any of the minor league films depicting terror by fire, earthquake, insects or alien invasions.

Americans no longer hesitate to admit they enjoy watching violence, or that it has become firmly entrenched in the American way of life. We need gut-grabbing thrills to keep going; happy events do not provide this sensation. Good news is dull. Most of our mass media would collapse financially if they were required to rely on good news for survival. Good news doesn't tingle the spine, raise the blood pressure, or squeeze the innards with a vise-like grip. Good news is welcome, but it lacks the power to maintain interest.

Though we decry violence on the highways, the increasing crime rate and the daily threat of war and riots, Americans seem obsessed with watching it in some form. These biggy films attract thousands, but even more people are content to stay home and watch a good western or police story on television.

"We tolerate poets but we love John Wayne," writes a columnist. Westerns are popular because they clearly depict the age-old struggle between good and evil with a good dose of violence thrown in. The good guys are always good and the bad guys are always bad, and each sticks to their role. The arm-chair viewer can identify with the fellow who fights for law and order and feel good about it. How he defends truth is incidental. He is a moral hero, though he carries a gun on his thigh and doesn't hesitate to use it.

I know I may bring violence upon my own head by suggesting that America's intense involvement with spectator sports is another indication of our passion for violence. The crowd roars, "Wipe 'em out," "Kill the umpire." These words mean nothing, the total fan tells me — just a figure of speech. Yet are they? Frederic Wertham in *A Sign of Cain* writes that figurative violence may be only verbal, yet it has psychological implications and represents a kind of ruthlessness in thought and feeling. This particular kind of violence invades many spheres of life; for example, the noise of loudspeakers in public places, the loud radio or stereo in private ones without regard for others in the vicinity. It appears in politics, economic life, art and literature and the ordinary relations between human beings. We are so enveloped by it we hardly realize it anymore.

Such psychological violence covers any kind of manipulation of one person by another so that he or she is not free to act. It includes written and oral propaganda, biased reports, advertising which pressures to buy and consume, and secret sessions of a committee who, by their private knowledge, have a form of power over the ones not included.

Why are we so obsessed with violence? Obviously we are

still the children of Cain in spirit and in act. Psychologist Joyce Brothers, responding to a feature article on *Jaws,* writes that we drain off some of our own fears by watching others suffer. Our own problems — whatever they may be — look mild in proportion to that of a person being mangled by a monstrous shark. To get this effect, each film has to be more horrifying than the one before.

We love and use violence because we haven't yet learned the lessons Christ was teaching his followers. Most people use violence when they face a situation in which they think they are right and the other person is wrong. They feel compelled to defend their position. They use it also as a reaction to someone who asserts they are right.

The way of violence is chosen by those who demand success at any price. Therefore, anyone who wants to help stem the tide of physical violence in the world must put forth great effort to escape the standardized ways of success-thinking, says Wertham.

Jesus spoke of how the "rulers of the Gentiles lord it over them, and their great men hold them in subjection." I get the feeling he was talking about clout, a popular word today in both Christian and secular circles. It refers to the person who can make things move by sheer weight of personality and position. When the followers of Jesus fought about who would be most important, he told them that whoever was the servant of all was the greatest. He taught them that the most effective clout was a washbasin and towel — not lobbying, or propagandizing, or using a fist.

In the political world, which may include the ecclesiastical realm, that kind of action doesn't make sense because it doesn't lead to quick success.

Evangelism
of the masses

20

Katie: *In the first thirty seconds of that television movie,
one man was killed and another was set up as a target for a
second killing.*

You: *If the first thirty seconds showed a woman forgiving
her husband for his unfaithfulness and the next scene showed
promise of more forgiveness, how many people would stay
tuned? Violence on television makes money, not peace.*

Katie: *But do we who watch remain untouched by what we
see?*

The loudspeaker at the discount store blared out that some
free samples of merchandise would be given away at a nearby
counter within a few minutes. I joined the shoppers who rushed
to share in this unexpected windfall.

I need not have hurried, for it took several long minutes
before the hefty salesman moved to his store podium to inform
us that his company was giving away as advertising samples a
new-type gold pen and pencil set valued at $5.95. The set
gleamed in his hand as he waved it before us.

But it wasn't ours yet. Fifteen minutes later we were still
waiting for our free gift while he prattled on about another pen
and holder set worth $2.95 which he was also going to give
away free. A little later he had the crowd raising and lowering
their hands in response to his appeals for advertising support

like a seasoned evangelist.

By then I had had enough. He had taken enough of my time and convinced me the hook was coming soon. No one gives away about $10 worth of merchandise for nothing. I walked away, disturbed at having been a sucker for this length of time.

Most thinking people brace themselves against the super-salesman. They look with suspicion upon the multitudinous health insurance folders stuffing the mailbox which promise "$150 per day while hospitalized." Mrs. Olson of television fame hasn't convinced them yet that her coffee is the "richest kind," nor the man who "ate the whole thing" that his antacid is the best.

They are wary of politicians who make whale-sized promises or evangelists who come on with a clearly manufactured charisma, a too-smooth delivery, and too many well-chiseled jokes.

All of the foregoing are openly propagandistic, so the readers and listeners have their guard up, ready to fend off the phony message, sometimes quite unmindful they are being evangelized by other forces without their conscious knowledge.

I was particularly aware of this recently as I studied various denominational periodicals. As I thumbed through issue after issue, looking for specific information, I was dimly aware that something was missing. It took me a while to figure out what was wrong.

Some of these church organs were written as if the only things that concerned its members either took place in the church building or on the mission field. That some staunch church members spend more time before the television set or at sports events than at church activities didn't enter the picture. The papers gave the impression that the world of public media didn't exist, or if it did, it didn't affect the readers of those magazines.

Yet it does.

Television, for example, has become part of the daily lives of most Americans, including Christians. It is now generally accepted that the average child spends 15,000 to 18,000 hours watching TV before he or she finishes high school — most of it quite willingly. If the child attends church about three hours per week, he or she spends about 2,500 hours there during the same period, some of it quite unwillingly.

Adults spend about as much time watching TV. Some slump before the set after a difficult day at work and let their brains shift into neutral while they watch a movie, sports event or talk show, unaware they are being evangelized to accept new attitudes to life, particularly those related to family, home and moral values. By repeating certain ideas again and again the mass media both affirm and confirm that their values are most acceptable. But the uncritical viewer or reader remains unconcerned, for it is only entertainment.

As one sifts through the mass of vulgarized material presented on television, it becomes apparent that one part of its gospel message is that the most important commodity a person has to give, sell or trade with another person is sex. It also teaches with great enthusiasm that the only sure way to settle difficulties, and certainly the most interesting way, is with violence. Peaceful people don't make good newspaper copy or exciting television heroes. How long would a TV show maintain its ratings if the good guy and the bad guy tried a little peaceful arbitration instead of a shoot-out? The experiences and language of faith and peace are dull stuff as TV program material.

My point: though we may never raise our hands in response to a TV commercial or walk down a sawdust trail to greet a talk show host, we may already be giving our allegiance to the gods of this world in greater measure than we realize. What happens in the church building or on the overseas mission station doesn't say it all.

Clustering

21

Katie: *I feel lonely and out of it tonight. I wish I had someone to talk to about that problem I had at school today.*

You: *You wouldn't want anyone to know you were really feeling down, would you?*

Katie: *Why shouldn't I let another person know I need help?*

You: *Well, there'd be gossip around the campus right away if you told anyone.*

Katie: *But I need someone.*

You: *Forget it, you'll get over it.*

I think often these days about my parents and the courage they and many others had to move from the Ukraine in Russia to Canada in 1923. The move forced them to change their lifestyle radically, even though they didn't know what a lifestyle was.

They left behind close relatives, friends and a familiar way of life because of deep-seated dissatisfactions with what they saw happening in their homeland. They risked everything to come to the new land, where they accepted the bondage of travel debts, the necessity to learn a new language and adapt to a new culture.

My parents tell me the first years in Canada, even before the Depression, were extremely cold and poor — but not unhappy. They lived with hope and love in a tiny two-room house we would probably call a shack today from the pictures I have seen of it. My parents and my two sisters slept in one room; my father's brothers in the kitchen. Before Mother could make the morning meal, they had to get up to give her room to work.

Mother remembers that each Sunday that year in Laird, Saskatchewan, the house filled with many other new immigrants who lived in worse housing. No one minded the meager fare they shared together. "We needed one another," Mother tells me. These strangers in a strange land leaned on one another for support during a difficult time of adjustment.

I think of those families and then of the numerous reports of the way today's nuclear families are self-destructing almost as fast as they are forming. Here today; gone tomorrow. Something within the very structure of the nuclear family makes it difficult to hold together. Some families are testing alternative models, with more cohesiveness, but as yet without too much success.

One alternative model with which a group at Packard Manse at Stoughton, Massachusetts, has been experimenting since 1961 is "clustering." It reminds me of the way my parents lived as newcomers to this land. A cluster, as opposed to a commune, is a group of families and individuals living in separate dwellings, sometimes separated by miles, but committed to each other for support and also to breaking down the patterns in society which separate people.

This group identifies a key factor in the breakup of the nuclear family as society pressures the family to become an independent unit. The "good" family today is self-sufficient — financially, emotionally and spiritually. One or two adults are solely responsible for the financial and emotional stability of the other members. If they fail because of health or other reasons, the alternative is public welfare or charity — both of which have negative connotations in our society.

Because each family is expected to be self-sufficient, it must become both a possessor and a consumer. Each family is expected to own its own car, lawn mower, washer and dryer and so forth. Sharing is not part of the plan for families who live next door to each other. "Neither a borrower nor a lender be" is the rule, even for Christians who are neighbors.

According to this group, another strong characteristic of the nuclear family is its tendency to isolate itself and its members from others, even within the family. Each child expects a separate room or at least a separate bed as his or her own right. To sleep with a sibling is considered too primitive.

Yet I remember fondly the good times we four sisters had in our small slant-roofed bedroom closely filled with two white, metal double beds and one dresser. Our only claim to personal rights was one drawer each in the dresser and our own heated stone, wrapped in old cloths, to keep our feet warm on a winter night.

My best memories are of huddling deep into the comforters for the nightly story-telling period before the one naked bulb was switched off. For a short while we struggled with *Pilgrim's Progress* as bedtime fare, thinking it might be good nourishment for our souls. But we soon discontinued that, for the made-up stories by my sister Frieda, whose imagination was never hampered by slant roofs, 40-degree-below weather, or flour-sack pajamas, had more attraction.

The Packard Manse group says the nuclear family pulls apart in other ways. Our society has removed from family groups the old, the single, the sick, the troubled, the dying, and any who deviate from the norm, such as the mentally retarded. We refuse to lean on others, but we also won't let others lean on us. Let the government and professionals look after such people. We shut the doors to openly sharing our needs, failures, guilt feelings, with one another. To expose even sincere emotions such as loneliness, weariness, discouragement, or doubt is out of the question. Fear has built high walls around each of us, but we are so good at hiding our feelings and pretending all is well, that even the walls must be guessed at. We attempt to show ourselves adequate, independent and self-sufficient. Yet these traits are not the characteristics of a cluster, or of people who need each other and who are willing to lean and be leaned on as the occasion demands.

The kind of dissatisfaction with religious and economic liberty which pushed my parents to make a major change is not the problem church families face today. Yet how much discontent with present weaknesses in family structures would it take to make a major change in lifestyle toward more deliberate caring? Who would be willing to pay that price?

Sleeping in the backseat

22

Katie: *I'm afraid when I think of the new year.*
You: *Why afraid?*
Katie: *I have so many big decisions to make, and no one to discuss them with.*
You: *But you're a grown-up woman now —*
Katie: *Yes, but I wish I were a child again, so I could go to Mom and Dad for help.*

I find it easy to identify with the Charlie Brown cartoon tacked onto my bulletin board. Lucy asks Charlie what he thinks security is. He replies that it is sleeping in the backseat of the car when you're a little kid. "You've been somewhere with your Mom and Dad, and it's night, and you're riding home in the car, and you can sleep in the backseat. You don't have to worry about anything . . . Your Mom and Dad are in the front seat and they do all the worrying . . . they take care of everything."

I often felt that security when, as a child, the seven members of our family, tightly packed into one small car, drove the long twenty miles home from church. As soon as the motor started, we children each borrowed a shoulder or a head for a pillow and dropped off. We didn't have to worry about a thing. We knew Mom and Dad in the front seat would stay awake while we slept.

But, as Charlie reminds Lucy, suddenly it's over, and you never get to sleep in the backseat again. Never. At some point that feeling of warm security slips away. Now it's up to you.

Listening to people discuss the problems facing the earth with threats of a population explosion, inflation, food and energy shortages, I feel as if some of them think the Moms and Dads in the front seat haven't been staying awake. The feeling of security during the last years of prosperity is lessening, and with the car salesman who hasn't made a sale in several weeks and facing a checkless month, they say, "I'm afraid."

Recession. Depression. Inflation. Stagflation. Whatever you call it, the present situation is forcing everyone to wake up, and most of us don't like it. Faith with prosperity and plenty felt a lot more comfortable and easy to get along with than faith without them may become. Suddenly both the front and backseats have made room for fear to travel alongside.

Today if you want to worry, you can pick your fears to measure like a suit of clothes on a discount rack. They abound like flies over rotting garbage on a warm summer day. People have become so insecure, anxious and bewildered that fear dominates their lives: fear of being burglarized or mugged; fear of children turning to drugs, drink or easy sex; fear of growing old, getting cancer, or dying; fear of body odor or a breakdown in the television on a holiday; fear of an accident on the highway; fear of corruption in government; fear of the cold impersonality of church life; fear of being bored at a meeting; fear of gaining weight; fear of buying a lemon of a car. . . .

The list can be extended almost infinitely.

All of us are afraid at some time. Bible characters were not exempt. David feared Saul and ran for his life. Hagar feared she and her son Ishmael might perish in the desert. Abram feared what the Egyptians might do to his wife Sarah. Jacob feared a meeting with his brother Esau even though God had promised to be with him. God knows we are fearful people.

Charlie Brown and Lucy had no solution to their sudden understanding of life other than to grasp one another's hands in desperation. When I sense worry is moving into step with me, I turn to Hannah Whitall Smith's *The Christian's Secret of a Happy Life*, written about 1870, for her formula for security for troubled times.

She suggests that the person who sees only the enemy and their horses and chariots, as did the servant of Elisha, pray that the Lord open his or her eyes to see that God has horses and chariots also, waiting to carry his children to places of victory. These horses and chariots are always present at every trial.

The next step is to learn to mount these chariots. This begins with recognizing that each trial which comes to us is actually God's chariot for us, an opportunity to lean on his strength. Whether we are troubled by suffering, trial, defeat, misunderstanding, disappointment or unkindness, God does not command or originate the matter, but the moment we put the fear or concern into his hands and accept it as from him, it becomes his and he turns it into a chariot of victory. Joseph was able to see his slavery and imprisonment in Egypt, not as the result of an act of hatred of his brothers, but as God working in his life. "God sent me before you," he said to them.

Mrs. Smith suggests we turn the tables on Satan. If we accept trials and worries as coming from our fellow human beings, they will defeat us, because then we must find our answers in people. If we can accept them as being allowed by God, then the one we have to answer to is God alone. We are free of conflict with other persons.

"Now I will lie down in peace, and sleep; for thou alone, O Lord, makest me live unafraid" wrote the Psalmist (4:8). Maybe he was thinking of the backseat of Mom and Dad's car when he penned those lines.

. . . about
freedom
to obey

A man
and a cross

23

Katie: *I saw a woman today with jewelled crosses for earrings! Crosses dangling from ears seem a far cry from Christ dangling from a cross of shame.*

You: *Maybe she screwed them real tight so that they'd hurt.*

Katie: *Real funny! But maybe her way is the only way a person can bear a cross today.*

I carry in my mind the picture of a man toiling up a hill, bearing a heavy cross. Writers like John Bunyan have etched that image indelibly into my mind, an image that fits another era better when people walked long distances and knew something about crosses, steep hills and climbing.

Cross-bearing and the automotive age don't match, for how would you get a cumbersome cross into a car? It would poke the back and front windows, scratch the vinyl upholstery, and crowd the driver and passengers, making it unsafe to drive.

The combination of man and cross don't fit into an airplane any better, for then the cross would have to be checked as baggage and would run the risk of being lost before it reached the carousel at the point of arrival.

In today's matched-decor, push-button home, which room could be used as the repository for the cross when the burden-bearer brings it home each evening? It wouldn't match the

wrought-iron patio furniture any better than the French pro-
vincial in the living room.

Cross-bearing in our time seems as out of place as a
primitive Indian in a loincloth making hors d'oeuvres in an
electronic kitchen. Instead of looking for a cross to bear, most
people look for something to bear their burdens — either a
machine, a pill, a drink, a movie or a television program.

Yet Christ said to his disciples, "If anyone wishes to be a
follower of mine, he must leave self behind; he must take up his
cross and come with me" (Mt. 16:24 *NEB*). To every person a
cross. Each his or her own cross. Not Christ's cross. In this
century. Each must choose to bear it. It is never thrust upon
one: "If anyone wishes. . . ."

I believe the meaning of the cross to the believer has
changed with the years. During the 1940s and 50s when L. E.
Maxwell's *Born Crucified* was popular in conservative Christian
circles, the cross meant going into missionary work overseas for
many people. If a person couldn't go personally, the cross could
be worked out by giving and praying for those who went.

Who can forget the full sanctuaries at mission conferences
resounding to "Send the light, send the light"? How many
mission prayer bands infiltrated Bible schools, church-related
colleges and church groups? Many Christ-followers built a rich,
meaningful life around these concepts, gladly giving time,
effort and money that the goals of mission programs might be
fulfilled. The missionary with pith helmut struggling with the
heat, insects and wild animals, while ministering to illiterate
savages matched the cross-bearing image.

Today, mission conferences and missionary reports, with
their departing airplanes and fading sunsets, have blended into
the general church landscape. And I fear the concept of the
cross of Christ has joined them.

Yet the words of Christ are still pertinent to us today. The
cross of Christ for the believer needs a radical redefinition in
this age which will identify the person with the death and
resurrection of Christ in other ways than a lapel pin, earrings or

a bumper sticker.

A. W. Tozer writes of the cross as the "overwhelming interference" of religion in the believer's life, the kind of interference
which directs the person away from the circular rabbit path
many choose to follow. Christianity never complicates a person's life on this narrow path. The people who tread it invite few
problems to themselves.

Who are some people who have dared to pick up a cross,
their cross? I think of the mother whose son is in prison because
of drug-related crimes. She continues to love him and pray for
him, but she has begun work with other young people involved
with drugs. It takes a new resurrection and a new strength to
get things going again when a world crumbles for a parent in
such a way.

I think of those who have taken up the challenge to bring
Christ and new hope to those in slums, prisons and under-
privileged areas. I think of those who have made their cross the
task of making room for oppressed minority groups such as
blacks, Chicanos, women, the poor and the old. Their path will
not be easy, for those who speak for the oppressed soon become
separated from those who choose the apparent security of the
rabbit path, which demands few decisions.

I think of those for whom the cross of Christ means
challenging the present political systems and also the way the
church has identified with American culture. That kind of
burden-bearing cannot be accomplished on a rabbit path either.

The kind of cross Christ spoke about was always a scandal,
never a pleasant pastime. No halo, no glory, no heroic martyr-
dom, was associated with it. Likewise, today, the person with a
cross faces daily dyings and resurrections to the world and the
world to him or her. That kind of cross-bearing requires full-
time effort. And it can take place in a car or an airplane — perhaps even on a bicycle or on foot.

The cross
and a bag
of potato chips

24

Katie: *Just once I'd like to discuss the sermon with other listeners right after I hear it. I go home and forget it until I hear a new one next week. It doesn't make sense.*

You: *Why don't you suggest having the church service before Sunday school?*

Katie: *It wouldn't work. Most of these people would get upset. Didn't you know that the time church begins and ends was established in heaven?*

I told a group of senior high students that one of the tasks of the church is to distinguish between the essence of the gospel and the culture which carries it. I felt good about my statement until one of them asked, "If it were possible to put the entire church with all its institutions, forms and rituals through a sieve to remove all cultural accretions, what would be left?"

The task I had set for those students was more difficult than I had realized at first.

If we could strip the gospel of all embellishments added by our American way of life, what would we find? What part of church life is the expression of faith? What part is the expression of American culture?

For some time now, the church has been criticized for being led by the nose by the culture of the times and for teaching the Word gilded by the Great American Dream, individualism, competition, progress and power. Instead of moving to the cutting edge of society and fighting sin where it is virile, the church has trailed behind comforting the wounded. It no longer speaks for truth and righteousness.

The Apostle Paul faced this problem of distinguishing between culture and Christianity in his ministry. When the Gentiles wanted to become Christians, he had to decide what was Jewish culture and what was necessary for faith in Jesus Christ. Should the Gentiles become Jews before they became Christians? Paul worked his way through that problem, even as we need to think through why the church today seems to require a God-seeker to become a respectable white middle-class citizen before he or she becomes a Christian.

However, before we make culture too much an enemy of the faith, we need to remind ourselves that faith will always attach itself to some kind of culture. Christianity has always found roots in some type of forms and institutions. In fact, it had little existence apart from Western culture until this century. Christianity has helped to shape American culture, which, in turn, now seems to be strangling it.

Because of the close connection between religion and culture, some people see the latter as the guardian of the faith, which, in turn, needs to be protected so it can keep the faith secure. I can remember when one congregation I worshiped with firmly believed that if the faith of our fathers was detached from the agricultural mode of living and the German language, all would be lost. Today most Mennonites have adopted an urban, middle-class way of life.

But again, I hear fears voiced that faith will be lost unless we can stick to our middle-class format with its large church buildings, paid clergy, extensive educational programs and well-dressed congregations and traditional forms of worship. That Christian truth might thrive — or even survive — without any of these is hard to grasp, for most of us like what we believe and practice at present.

Middle-aged Christians have their own clear idea of what the Bible teaches, frequently determined by who the strongest teachers and preachers were during their youth. Their biases became truth for their followers. For example, dispensationalism dominated the religious world when I was a young adult. I recall the intense discussions we enjoyed about premillennialism, eternal security and predestination. We had our proofs in the three-point outlines of our teachers.

Over the years I also accepted that Christians were to keep their distance from good works, for this practice smacked of the social gospel. Further, the most important text, next to John 3:16, was Matthew 28:18. The command to go to "all nations" meant anyone in an overseas country, not people living close by. Giving to the Lord meant giving to missions, not to the drunk down the street.

Such views are hard to give up, for they seem right and biblical.

Yet today, though most people agree overseas missions must continue, the emphasis in evangelism is shifting to the inner city here in the homeland. Increasing numbers of Christian leaders reiterate that Christ identified with the poor and oppressed, and if the church is to be the body of Christ, it must also identify with the poorest, weakest, most abused members of society. It must become a church of the poor — poor in spirit and poor in worldly goods. Christ gave the believer a cross, not an arm chair, a bag of potato chips and a TV. Yet this concept doesn't fit the view of today's church as a progressive, wealthy institution meeting the Sunday needs of middle-class Americans.

As I think over my adult years, I find that the greatest pain in my spiritual pilgrimage has been regarding the necessity to change my mind about what I was sure the Bible taught. I recognize now that at times the American culture has spoken as loudly to me as the Bible and has determined my thinking without my being aware of it because the church promoted these truths. To make the truth of Scripture preeminent in life and thought is difficult — no doubt about it.

Why? Because a church is always a church in a culture, not out of it. It should not be led by it, but should lead it. The church does not fit God and his Word into its agenda and schedule, but yields itself to him. And there's the hitch. We all have a lot of Watergate clinging to our heels. Things seem to go better with compromise.

So it's important to know the difference between Christianity and culture for a simple reason — to be able to rise above it, if need be, to fulfill God's commands.

Abraham lived within his culture when he lied about Sarah and also when he agreed to have a child by her maid. He lived above the culture when he heard God speaking to him and followed his leading out of the Ur of Chaldees.

David lived within his culture when he commanded Bathsheba to come to him. As king he could demand this of any woman. He lived above his culture when he sought God's pardon for the sin of adultery and for causing the death of Uriah.

So scrape away, Holy Spirit, at unwanted and unnecessary accretions. Even though it hurts.

Time
for the living

25

Katie: *She told me she hadn't stopped to see me because she thought I would be busy.*
You: *Too bad, for you weren't busy last night.*
Katie: *I know. But I let people think I am.*

The close relative of a friend died. She left work to attend the morning funeral service. In the afternoon she was back for a meeting. I expressed surprise at her soon return.

"Too much work to do here," she responded gloomily. Life left her no time to mourn the dead, unlike an earlier era when a death curbed family activities, sometimes for several months. I would not want to bring back those customs, yet if we have no time for the dead, do we have time for the living?

Time obviously fascinates us. I look with some apprehension and yet amazement at the complicated devices called wristwatches on the arms of some persons. Attached are full calendars, stop watches, alarm devices, second-hand readouts, and much, much more. Time is watched, guarded, captured, controlled, overcome and sometimes killed.

Though humankind has made much technological advance, the control of time still eludes us. So we work to squeeze in another activity by evading a different one or by shunting activities. Even punctuality, once a highly prized virtue, is suffering as more and more busy people forego the preliminaries of a meeting (introductory comments, singing, prayer) and settle for just the talk, sermon or discussion. To outwit time has become the main preoccupation of many busy persons.

Sometimes I wake up at night with a start wondering whether the church of tomorrow will have to fight the battle of the calendar like we do today. Church pillars run around with an engagement book in their vest pocket or purse. The little book tells them where they should be at what time, what place, and what for. Discipleship shifts to the nitty-gritty when it comes to the little book.

Date books which began the year clean and fresh look pocket- and purse-worn by October. Too seldom do I see anyone bring one out with joy. More often the sight of the little book produces the long and tired look, as the person pencils in one more slot — like a bingo card. I watched a friend fill in another blank. He was a whopping big winner this month. Nearly every square was covered. He could soon holler "Bingo" and claim his prize.

Another time, I discovered I hadn't yet seen the ultimate in date books. Beside the person next to me lay a Six-year Planner! I shuddered. Does *God* even have my life programmed that far ahead? What is the prize for having captured time by means of a little black book or wristwatch? Have we trapped time, or has time trapped us?

I find we like to talk a lot about time and our conflict with it, and especially how to find time for other people and church ministries. I sense we all struggle with two conflicting philosophies regarding the use of time — both of which claim to have biblical foundations.

The one voice is similar to the title of the booklet before me: "Time Is Money, Don't Waste It." The Bible warns against laziness, so Christians are urged to "Redeem the time, for the days are evil." Work has more value than play. Each minute must be filled with purposeful, productive activity.

Read a book on the bus. Write letters while listening to a lecturer. Knit at a meeting. Meet with committee members over meals. Dictate letters while driving. Prepare notes for a lecture while listening to one. Jot a memo to someone while answering the phone. Total disgrace is to be caught in reverie, contemplating a dead leaf twirling across the highway.

Such utilitarian attitudes toward work and time seem good. As young people we were admonished from the pulpit to "burn out for God" and to "spend and be spent" to get God's blessing. To be wholly yielded to God meant to be aggressively engaged in Christian activity every waking moment — regardless of the cost to family and self. Jesus was first, others second, and self last.

Today another voice is competing with this one. It shouts "Slow down and live. You've got a lot of living to do." What are the opportunities the Christian is expected to redeem? What coinage does he or she use to make this barter? Did the Apostle Paul expect people to sacrifice personal growth, home life and friends to remain true to him?

This second voice urges you to learn to say no, for no one will look after your health if you don't. You aren't indispensable to any organization. Jog a little. Play tennis. Enjoy the sunset. Take care of your relationships. Make room for spouse and children. To burn out for God may have been valid for persons like Judson and Taylor, but such sacrifice doesn't make sense in this age. You are responsible for self and family because you are a creation of God.

So what shall it be? Get God's work done at the sacrifice of family relationships, or keep the family together and let those who will, keep the church program going?

Each person will have to find his or her own answer to the matter of sanctifying time, yet a few principles are worth mentioning. The first is that God never gives a person more to do than he or she can handle. Let's encourage the congregation, whom we expect to help members live whole lives, take the first step by being less concerned about getting workers to fill positions in church programs than about being sure these workers are doing what God wants them to do. This action

might play havoc with some of the spur-of-the-moment elec-
tions which drag people into activities without warning, but it
might also help some people from having to pray for their
second wind when they have taken on more than they can
handle.

Michael Quoist in *The Meaning of Success* points out that
if you've been told several times, "Oh, I didn't dare to disturb
you the other day . . . you looked so busy," to watch out. Such
words, he says, are a serious warning because many other
people have likely come and gone away without having talked
to you. He adds that if you don't have enough time to get
everything done, stop for a moment to pray. "Then place your
work before God as you do it. What you can't finish, leave, even
if others become insistent and refuse to understand, for God has
not given you this work to do."

Second, I think if we realized anew that life is bounded
by death, not by the alarm clock or the calendar, time might
move into clearer perspective. Most of us get more than our
allotted three score years and ten before we die. We have time
to grow up, to go to school, to marry and raise families, to make
friends, to have careers and change them, to worship and serve
God, to be old and die. What more do we want?

Last, we must remember that unless we grasp the significance of time and learn how to make it holy, we suffer. To kill
time either by being too busy or not busy enough is to be killed
by it. To pack too much living into each minute or to endure the
passing of the clock is to be time's slave.

Time will never be killed off. To attempt to do so is to
commit suicide, for time is life. It is only in time that we find out
who we are. It is only in time that we make a friend. It is only
in time that we meet God. These things happen now — in the
moment of grace — when we take time for them.

A person's date book is his or her creed. Whatever one
takes time for is what one believes in. So, as the preacher in
Ecclesiastes said, there is time for everything. If I can't look
ahead into the day with joy and thanks to God that there will be

enough time for him and his Word, for family, for those with burdens and those without, I think I should throw away my date book and start again.

If, on the other hand, I have lost all sense of bonding with God's people and believe that I can go it alone as a Christian, it may be time to buy a date book and use it. And make the first appointment one with God.

The
luxury
of isolation

26

Katie: *Every time I look at that fellow in the next pew with his straggly hair and fragile beard, I have to swallow hard — as if a grasshopper got stuck in my throat.*

You: *Why does he bother you? God doesn't worry about his hair and beard, so why do you?*

Katie: *I like my Christians neat and tidy — not looking like molting sheep!*

A reader took serious issue with an article in which I quoted from the *New English Bible*. God wrote only one Bible, he wrote me, and those words which differ from the *King James Version* aren't God's words. If I were a born-again Christian, I would recognize this, he admonished me.

I do not intend to discuss the authenticity of the newer versions of the Bible. Much abler Bible scholars than I have already done that often. I am glad, however, that the Christian church did not fixate on some versions older than the *King James Version*. We would have been in real trouble trying to figure out "*Fader ure, thu the eart on heafonum. Sin thin nama gehalgod. . . .*"

My concern is for the person who finds it hard to accept anyone as a Christian who does not duplicate his or her thinking, and who considers such people dangerous who make others aware that God has not and does not limit himself to one set of words (specifically, the *King James Version*), and one way of worshiping him (American conservative evangelicalism).

My switch to using some of the newer versions was not an unpremeditated act. It was one step in a longer series of deliberate changes I made in my spiritual pilgrimage, away from the comfort of formulations and definitions and prescriptions about Christ and his Word.

Someone has said we should always be suspicious of one who knows God too well, who calls him by his first name, for a human being cannot comprehend all of God, nor the ways of God. The nature of God holds infinite mystery. Yet some people have the matter of their relationship to God licked. They ask casually, "How's the Lord treating you these days?" as if he were a pal resting in the top bunk. To completely understand God and to be able to reduce him to formulas is to make him peanut-size. To accept the mystery of godliness, even while committing oneself to such light as one has received is to allow God to be God.

Some of my first spiritual stretching occurred when I was forced to acknowledge that the Christian world is larger than my Mennonite Brethren cocoon. I had always thought there were Mennonite Brethren and then there were others, and somehow, by some strange fluke, my kind of Christian had an edge on God's bounty.

One day I came up gasping for breath. I had been thrown into a pond which contained Christians of all kinds. I had to recognize there were Christ-believers among Baptists, Presbyterians, Methodists, Catholics and other kinds of Mennonites — or retreat behind a wall of my own construction and set up my defenses to keep others out.

Years later, as I was visiting with a young woman of another Mennonite branch, she remarked, "I'm so glad there're Christians in your denomination also." My mind did a sudden somersault. She, too, had the same problem? It became clear to me that in setting up our boundaries for defining Christians, we have institutionalized separation and alienation instead of becoming agents of reconciliation.

But accepting that there were Christians in other denominations was only Step One. Step Two was harder. That was to accept that there are other ways of coming to God than by walking down the aisle at a revival meeting or camp meeting to the chorus of "Just as I am, without one plea." Conversion is just as valid if one accepts Christ within the privacy of one's room. One does not need to have a notarized certificate giving the time, date and place of conversion to make it authentic. The true witness is in the heart and life.

Every time my world expanded, I feared, for each time I had to reconsider my previously learned set of formulas for testing Christianity. I could no longer judge a person by denominational affiliation, by the kind of Bible he or she read, or even by the kind of religious language used. The latter test was the most difficult to throw out, for it was such a convenient way of spotting true believers. To acknowledge to myself that these were not valid differences between Christians and non-Christians seemed to be giving in to the enemy.

Reconciliation is what the church is about, not division. When we line ourselves up with causes and preach personal biases instead of Jesus Christ, we lose those people who aren't interested in joining our little Society for the Preservation of the Clean-shaven Look, or for the Preservation of a Wooden-pew Church, or for the Prevention of Wearing of Wigs to Church, etc., etc. Causes need protection. Christ does not.

What did the Apostle Peter, a Jew, feel when he landed in Macedonia and found Cornelius, a Gentile, waiting for him? If he was troubled, he overcame the hurdle and accepted the Gentile as a brother. Out of this experience came his ringing words found in Acts 10:34, "Of a truth, I perceive God is no respecter of persons. In every nation he that feareth him, and worketh righteousness is accepted of him." I like the *King James Version* here.

So if a person calls him or herself a Baptist and fears God and works righteousness, that person is accepted of God.

Likewise if the denominational label is Mennonite or Presbyterian or Catholic.

If such are accepted of God, can we afford the luxury of isolation and separate ourselves from them? Christ prayed that his followers might be one. That prayer remains unanswered unless we show this oneness and come together in spite of our differences.

Cause or call?

27

Katie: *Where should I go tonight — to church to learn something about the problems of famine in Cambodia, to the school program to hear my children perform, to the meeting that wants to start an organization for single parents, or stay home and do the laundry?*

You: *This may be the only time you'll get a chance to hear about Cambodia. The need over there is unspeakable at present. That cause needs your support.*

Katie: *Is a need always a call? If so, do I listen to the one who shouts loudest? My kids will be going to school tomorrow in their nightgowns if I don't head for the laundromat.*

In my files I have a small clipping from an old newspaper about Tom Dooley, the American doctor and writer who worked in Vietnam prior to the war. He made history because of the quality and quantity of his work. Before he died at age 34, he had moved mountains in Vietnam to bring medical help to the tribespeople who would never have received it otherwise.

I keep the clipping about Dooley because it attempts to figure out what made him great. He lived with a sense of purpose. He knew he had a job to do. Given two people with the same talents and opportunities, one will accomplish much during a lifetime; the other will only wait for each day to end. The one with a sense of destiny or calling makes a meaningful pilgrimage of life; the other puts in time each day.

As I study the biographies of great leaders of the church, I find they carried within themselves this same clear sense of purpose. The late Orie Miller (Mr. MCC) was a man with a clear sense of calling from God. C. F. Klassen, another Mennonite Central Committee worker, who toiled tirelessly in Europe to bring Mennonite refugees to safety after World War 2, shared this feeling. Some missionaries, ministers and laypeople have it; others merely work.

How one gets this sense of purpose varies. Some people are pulled along in life by a desire for riches, others by a longing to be well known or to have power, and still others by the pressure to gain social status. When such persons die, their obituary does not read like Tom Dooley's. Howard J. Hughes, who died one of the world's wealthiest men, blessed few people while he lived, especially in his latter years.

Why do some people have this clear inner call and others stumble aimlessly through life? Is it that persons like Dooley and Miller were born at the right time and then matched the circumstances which drew greatness out of them? Possibly. This view has validity, yet I cannot accept it completely.

I believe that persons with a sense of destiny started with the knowledge that God wanted them. Yet God's call is not necessarily to a specific task; it is first of all to him. God did not address his call to Isaiah personally: God asked, "Who will go for us?" Isaiah was within hearing distance and responded. Whether or not we hear God's call depends on the state of our ears, writes Oswald Chambers. God's call is to everyone, but only those who have the nature of God in them hear and respond.

But this doesn't mean that people aren't hearing calls. Not at all. Loud, sometimes blatant appeals for loyalty and money come from all kinds of causes, ideologies, false gods and images. These get mixed up with the call of God because they are frequently a call to something good and worthwhile. Those who have hurried to get membership buttons, thinking they have heard God's call, wonder why later on the slogans and jingles begin to jangle. They find they have joined a system of causes and good works without the power of the Spirit and which has no particular relationship to the gospel except in name.

By this I do not mean to say that we can evade or retreat from the great issues affecting humankind these days, such as hunger, oppression, violence. Yet the supernatural call of God is a response first of all to him. Service is the outflow of our devotion to him. The compulsion to work to erase hunger from the world's surface comes from a relationship to Christ, not a pressure to wave banners, shout and parade for a particular cause.

All of this may sound very elemental. Of course, every worker in the church or its institutions should know he or she is called by God. Yet in the urgency of the tremendous needs of humankind today, people are pressured to respond to causes, often very good causes. At times I feel pulled to pieces, not knowing where to give my time and loyalty.

I also think that the crisis in leadership in our congregations relates to this decreasing emphasis on the call of God. In the past, leaders emerged from the ranks of the congregations as God's gifts; charisma was apparent in them. Today the church tends to look for professionals who have expertise in public work or administration and who exude a sparkling personality. Yet an overemphasis on such qualities tends to dilute and dissolve a consciousness of the call of God.

What makes this sense of purpose even more difficult to talk about openly is expressed in Chambers' statement: "It is easier to serve God without a vision, easier to work for God without a call, because then you are not bothered by what God requires; . . . you will be more prosperous and successful, more leisure-hearted, if you never realize the call of God."

So once again I put the clipping about Tom Dooley back into the file to yellow a little while longer. Does one dare talk about such matters in a society concerned about prosperity and success?

The invisible poor

28

Katie: *I'd really like to help the poor, but out here in Kansas, where nearly everyone is middle-class, I rarely see a poor person.*

You: *You don't see them because you don't want to see them. I bet there are as many poor in Kansas, even in Hillsboro, as this community could help.*

Katie: *Yes, but where are they?*

You: *What about the family across the street?*

Katie: *That's the deacon's job to help them. Anyway, they belong to the other church.*

One day I walked into our classroom at school — I must have been about ten or eleven — to see one of the poorest girls in the community wearing the same dress as mine. Both were made of yellow cotton printed with tiny green flowers. What added to the discomfort was that Mother had made both of them. Mine was my own. She was wearing my older sister's hand-me-down.

Even today I remember how difficult it was to figure out my feelings that morning. Though we were poor during the Depression, other families were poorer, and social classes existed. Running to another home with a bundle of outgrown clothes seemed the right thing to do, but being identified with the poor by wearing the same dress seemed too much. I didn't like her standard of living and mine being the same if we weren't the same kind of poor. I realize now we need the poor. They give the rich a higher rung on the social ladder to stand on.

With the number of poor increasing here as well as in other countries, Christian leaders are asking us to be more aware of them. A study of both the Old and New Testaments shows that God is on the side of the poor, the powerless and the oppressed, and that he resists the rich, the powerful and proud. Despite this emphasis, the interest in the cause of the poor is weak. Why?

In rethinking my childhood experience, I think I have stumbled on one reason why the cause of the poor lags. Unlike the poor of previous decades who were always before our eyes in our communities, the millions of poor in the United States today are invisible. And out of sight means out of mind.

Without much effort I can recall several experiences with the poor of my childhood which aroused the compassion of at least the adults. One day Father came home from the store where he worked to tell us that a man had come in early that morning asking for an empty wooden sardine crate. During the night his wife had given birth to a stillborn infant. He needed something to bury it in. Packing crates were the cheapest coffins.

Another time the local teachers investigated the persistent theft of school lunches and tracked the misdeed to a young boy who lived with his grandmother. He was severely whipped. Later someone thought to investigate the home. They found his grandmother's cupboard bare. The boy stole because he was hungry. Then even grown men wept.

I remember clearly the rough-looking hoboes who rode the rails, stopping in our community to beg a handout or a meal at the door. Mother gave what she could while we children watched this unshaven stranger consume the food.

"Across the tracks" falls flat today as a joke. Many of the younger generation don't know what it means. Although we children had our laughs about the phrase, we knew that the homes at the far edge of town were smaller and less substantial than our frame structures.

Today "across the tracks" is an unknown place to middle-class citizens. Popular tourist routes don't direct traffic through the ghetto. People are unaware of the poor because they don't make interesting news copy. The poor don't get elected to leadership positions, nor do they make decisive speeches so they can be quoted. In the church they are the people one does things *for* rather than *with*. They become a project rather than people with whom one has a close relationship.

Michael Harrington in *The Culture of Poverty* writes that the development of America has removed poverty from the living, emotional experience of millions upon millions of its middle-class citizens. The poor are invisible, he says, because they live off the main tracks. They are the wrong age to be seen — many are sixty-five years of age or older, or under eighteen. Others are sick and cannot move. Another group live out their lives in loneliness and frustration in rented rooms — out of sight and out of mind — and alone. Their poverty is not seen. They are poor because they were poor; they stay poor because they are poor. They live in a culture of poverty.

Today I wish I had been gracious enough to say to the little girl in the yellow dress like mine, "I like being dressed the same as you." At the time I couldn't find the words. That is still the problem. People can prove to us that the poor exist by means of statistics, pictures and articles, but until they become visible to us and we are willing to identify with their needs as Christ did, they will not seem real. The tendency will be to assure ourselves someone else is taking care of them.

What kind
of good news?

29

Katie: *Christianity in America is basically a rich, white man's religion. Much of what makes up your Christian life couldn't be part of a poor person's daily life.*

You: *That's not true.*

Katie: *Well then, start fitting the Christian aspects of your life into that of a woman with six children living in a two-room cold-water apartment on a very small fixed income. List the highlights of the Christian life in such a situation and what you consider important now.*

You: *Books, magazines, time for fellowship with friends, opportunity for some kind of service, travel to workshops, . . .*

Some days I feel sorry for my postman. Along with the letters I welcome, he carries junk mail to my mailbox by the front door. I bring it in the house and then carry it to the garbage can by the back door. Sometimes the transaction takes only a few minutes.

Never has so much paper been sent to so many by so few, urging readers to subscribe. A special magazine or newsletter is available for every aspect of the Christian life: business, missions, aging, youth, students, charismatics, social justice, evangelism, medical arts, leadership, creative arts, theology, history, psychology, athletics, politics, charm and many more.

I'm a strong believer in the written word, but as I look over some magazines, I sense many are slanted toward the affluent reader — the Christian with enough money to live, not the abundant Christian life, but the "good Christian life."

If some publisher were to consider issuing a magazine exclusively for the poor — the hungry, defeated, miserable people who live in slums, shantytowns and refugee camps, what would he put in it? Christ said he came to preach good news to the poor (Mt. 11:5). What was that good news? How would such a magazine differ from what satisfies the reading appetites of the rich?

I found it easier to check off what would have to be left out of such a magazine rather than what would be included. First, such a magazine wouldn't need articles encouraging people to attend workshops, seminars and institutes in distant cities to learn anything from management skills and successful church leadership to raising money for the Lord's work.

You can't go to such functions if you haven't the money to **register in hotels and motels advertised at $60 for double accommodations and $35 for single and $14.50 for the closing** banquet. Articles about conferences and conventions in similar settings which assure spiritual growth and fellowship would probably fall into the same category. The rich can't survive without them, but the poor Christian has to.

Articles about prayer breakfasts "continuing the custom Christ began" at which those present eat "mushroom quiche and spicy beef sausage" while listening to "spirited calls for dependence on Christ" would also be out of place. Even a fish and rolls breakfast would be too expensive for the person whose pockets are empty.

Articles about Christ-centered retirement plans (where to find the best and most comfortable Christian fellowship in old age) and about wills, annuities and estate planning would fall into the same category. Not needed.

So would articles and ads encouraging readers to combine Bible conferences with Disneyworld, Hawaii and Bermuda cruises, which allow time for Bible study and prayer in the morning and cruising, cycling, golf, tennis, fishing, sailing and horseback riding the rest of the day.

Throw out also articles and ads for Christian charm courses for the woman who isn't doing all she can to enhance her natural beauty by the skillful use of makeup. One article I scanned said, "I've learned the art of easing out the wrinkles with cream, using a little color to brighten my eyes and cheeks, and it makes a difference in how I look and feel." Probably true, but only people with a regular income can afford to improve their self-image by beautifying their exterior image.

Of course, the editor of a magazine for the poor would omit material which advocates consuming less and enjoying it more and how to lose weight for the Lord. These admonitions would be unnecessary, as would articles on family living which insist it is impossible to raise children well unless each child has a private room, or at least a single bed.

So what would such a magazines include? Test these ideas: How to live the victorious life on a poverty budget; how to cook nutritious meals without enough food to do so; how to keep children happy without toys; how to keep pride from being wounded when forced to ask for help; how to keep dreams alive; how to trust the Lord when you're freezing cold.

Or look at it from another angle. If you were asked to explain the good news to a family of eight living in a drafty two-room cabin on a near-starvation diet, what would you say? Could you say something to them before speaking to yourself first?

Sitting close

30

Katie: *I can remember the first time I sat close to a black person — I was grown up too — but I knew it was a first.*

You: *How'd you feel?*

Katie: *I don't know — different — I knew I was supposed to feel different.*

You: *Maybe it was the first time he sat close to a Mennonite! Did you wonder how he felt?*

During the height of the race riots in the late sixties I made a purchase in an area of Wichita, our nearest big city, which I seldom frequent. To return to a more familiar street I decided to shortcut through the section populated mostly by blacks. I hesitated before I left the smooth pavement for the rutty, graveled road. I hadn't expected such roads in the middle of a large city.

As my car sped through the streets, I wondered what it feels like to be different from the majority. Most parents have had some unpleasant experiences they would not want their children to have. But what must it be like to know you are considered second-class; and though you can bear the slights, to know your children face the same prospects, sometimes for a lifetime.

How deep are the resentments and frustrations of people

who are discriminated against? The neighborhood in which I drove that afternoon looked peaceful enough. The houses gradually improved in appearance from squalid little shacks to respectable dwellings. Carefree children roamed the lawns and near-lawns. A group of happy black women enjoyed an afternoon visit under the sparse shade of a small tree. Was this the type of ghetto that had spawned the outbreaks of fighting in Cleveland or the riots in Detroit? Or were the people here as afraid of open conflict as the whites?

Even if they wanted no part of rioting, did they, perhaps somewhere deep underneath, have the feeling of the little girl in Mississippi who, after she had drawn a picture of herself, said, "That's me, and the Lord made me. When I grow up my momma says I may not like how he made me, but I must always remember that he did it, and it's his idea. So when I draw the Lord he'll be a real big man. He has to be to explain about the way things are."

God's idea that people are black? Yes. But God's idea that they should be looked down upon? How are the ambassadors of God's love going to explain that?

A student described her attitudes toward blacks as a child.

"You were afraid of being touched by a black person?" a friend asked her. "That's ridiculous."

"But I was."

"How about a time when a black person touched you? What did you think?"

"Well, I haven't thought too much about it. I guess I didn't want to remember. Yes, I was afraid . . . afraid I would be doomed forever, or my own skin would be changed from shock, or I would get some incurable disease. It could have been I was afraid I would die."

Language has abetted the attitudes of the whites in keeping the blacks burdened by a sense of inferiority. Although we think of language as the dress of our thoughts, linguists are proving that language itself shapes our thoughts and culture.

The words we use determine our thinking and our life.

According to *Roget's Thesaurus*, the word "whiteness" has about 134 synonyms, 44 of which are favorable; for example, purity, bright, shining, fair, clean. Only ten synonyms for whiteness have negative connotations: whitewash, ashen, gray. The word "blackness" has about 120 synonyms; 60 of these are decidedly unfavorable, and none of the others are really positive. To blacken something always means to denigrate it or make it of lesser value. Because we have no words for black which produce pleasant associations, anyone who uses English is forced to think of things black with repugnance and anything white with favor.

Children quickly learn to associate black with sin and evil. **The devil and the bogey-man are black, as are witches and their cats, mourning clothes, dirt, crows and niggers.**

All children in evangelical churches learn early that hearts are very, very black with sin before they are washed clean by the blood of Christ. This is one of the main points in the Wordless Book, an aid in evangelizing children. But biblical it is not. I can find no instance of sin being termed black in the Bible. Isaiah 2:18 says, "Though your sins be scarlet, they shall be as white as snow; though they be red like crimson, they shall be as wool."

It would overthrow many well-worked-out stories to pic- **ture sin to children like a gleaming red fire engine, a police car or a red cherry on a sundae instead of like** soot on the bottom of a pan, a thundercloud, coal or mud. The color red has too many pleasant connotations in our society. Yet Christ used "white," which also has many favorable connotations to depict the hearts of the sin-hardened Pharisees. He called them "whited sepulchres." The problem of our language is part of the intricate problem of racism from which the black man sees little escape until the concept "blackness" itself is redeemed in our language.

I feel assured that many Christians can honestly confess

they have no prejudice against minority races. This is particularly true where no unpleasant incidents have marred their
relationship. Yet, in spite of professed love for minorities, few
speak out against the inequities. It is difficult to do so without
being labeled a social gospeler.

At the pool of Bethesda a sick man waited with a multitude
of ailing folk for many years. Help had not come to these sick
people from the usual sources. Now they waited for the
opportunity to be the first to jump in when the angel moved the
water and be healed.

The sick man, who had kept to his bed for 38 years, had no
one to help him into the water. The people with the ingrown toe-
nails or a bad case of sunburn got there first. Or those who had
many friends and relatives. Jesus saw the man's need and
healed him. Not until later in the day did he direct his attention
to the man's inner need. His social action deeply offended the
Jews. They were upset and spoke out loudly against Jesus'
sweeping rejection of religious tradition. They feared for their
places of power and influence with the Jewish people. By their
words they showed they were bound as surely as the paralyzed
man. They were straitjacketed by a system; he by a physical
sickness. This story of the sick man by the pool in Jerusalem is
one of the most cutting exposés of a religion that had lost its
power.

As I study the Gospels I cannot shut my eyes to the fact
that Jesus had a keen eye for the physical and social needs of
the people of his day. Though we may not like to think of him as
such, he was a socio-political-religious figure. People in political
and religious leadership were disturbed by his actions.

Segments of the evangelical church are equally afraid that
they will be pushed into social action and that the gospel will
be left out. Evangelism, they state, should be the only real
concern of Christians and meeting other needs only incidental
— yet how incidental was the healing of the paralyzed man to
his later conversion? Let's thank those involved with social

action for helping us rediscover the human race as people with human needs. But who will help us regain confidence in the gospel which Christ lived and preached?

What might happen if blacks and whites got close to one another? Who knows, we might break out with love and understanding, and that's not a bad illness to suffer from.

While making gravy

31

Katie: *What if the man had turned on me and threatened to smash my face too, what should I have done then?*
You: *I don't know — probably run for your life!*

One evening as I was preparing supper, I looked out the window to see a middle-aged man forcing a young high-school-age girl into his car. When she resisted, his fist smashed into her face. Though uncertain what I was going to do, I rushed outside.

By then a neighbor was running ahead of me toward the man and girl. He shouted to the molester to quit abusing the girl, who had fallen to her knees. Startled by the sudden appearance of my neighbor, the man jumped into his car and backed down the street. At the same time friends of the girl picked her up in another car and indicated to us the incident was a family quarrel.

I went back to my gravy-making, thinking some deep thoughts about involvement. I think I was glad my neighbor had also seen the incident. If he hadn't been there, would my voice have been loud enough to stop the man's actions? If my words hadn't stopped him, what would I have done?

How much would I have been willing to risk for the sake of the girl, someone I had never seen before? How loudly would I have been willing to speak and act in her defense, especially in a family affair, traditionally off limits to outsiders?

I still don't know the answer to these questions.

Though most of us are rarely faced with breaking up a fistfight, I decided while stirring the lumps out of the gravy that the challenge to become a spokesperson or an advocate for another person is a daily opportunity. That's what Christianity is all about. Like Christ, who spoke up for the weak and defenseless against the powerful Pharisees, each day we need to counter evil in all forms, in social structures or in individual problems. A Christian must be an advocate.

The word "advocate" sounds stuffy. Maybe that's why we don't use it more. In ancient times, it was used with two related meanings. Demosthenes, the orator, used it to designate friends who voluntarily stepped in and personally urged the judge to decide in favor of their friend. Christ is this kind of an advocate even now. "If any man sin, we have an advocate with the Father, Jesus Christ the righteous," wrote the Apostle John.

Another common meaning of the word in Bible times was "one called to another's side to aid him." In the early church, the deacons were called to act as spokesmen for the widows who were not getting enough to eat at the distribution centers. Today deacons are still expected to be staunch advocates of the weak.

As I continued to think about the street incident, I concluded that we tend to think of oppressed people mostly as those who get mugged. However, oppression comes in many other guises we don't recognize. Ralph Nader is well liked by the ordinary consumer because he recognizes consumer oppression. Their lemon is also his lemon.

Why did Martin Luther King, Jr., gain such a following? Because he acted as a spokesman for a powerless people. Why is Common Cause gaining appeal? Because this national lobby speaks for the ordinary citizen who finds corrupt political practices too big a foe to fight alone. The newer programs for the mentally ill and the retarded are incorporating the principle of advocacy — of being a spokesperson for those who cannot defend themselves. Gloria Steinem has followers because she articulates for some women what they cannot say for themselves. She offers them hope for change. The newer journalism, also called advocacy journalism, purports to speak more clearly for the people by offering them background and interpretation instead of sterile objectivity.

Everyone needs an advocate at some time, whether it is just a friend who will persuade the plumber to make a call at your house to fix a stopped drain or someone to write a job recommendation. The ones who need an advocate worst are the sick, the blind, the elderly, the unborn, the orphaned, the defrauded, the rejected — they need a defender in the same way Christ defends us before the throne of God.

Persons who can't hear the words "social action" without looking for an Alka-seltzer might try using the word "advocate" instead. Some of the heroes in the halls of faith in Hebrews 11 won their place because they "overthrew kingdoms, established justice and saw God's promises fulfilled" (v. 33). They were advocates — persons who speak and act on Christ's behalf for the person who has no courage or power to keep going.

But if becoming an advocate might mean a fist in my face, would I be willing? By the time my thinking had progressed that far, it was time to eat supper. Maybe tomorrow I'd have another chance to think about the matter and do something about it . . . if I didn't go shopping.

. . . about
the language
of faith

The language event

32

Katie: *Which are more important in the life of faith, words or deeds?*

You: *I'd say deeds deriving from faith in Christ.*

Katie: *But you mean an act, don't you? Can words be a form of works or deeds, also?*

You: *What do you mean?*

Katie: *Like when you say "I promise . . .," or "I nominate Jane for. . . ."*

As a young person of about 19, I remember one Saturday, while in a frustrated mood, looking through a shelf of old books in the sunroom of the home where I was living. I came upon Oswald Chambers' *My Utmost for His Highest.* More out of curiosity than interest, I picked up the book of devotional readings and took it to my room to read the excerpt for the day: "'Ye shall be holy; for I am holy' (1 Pet. 1:16). Continually restate to yourself what the purpose of your life is. The destined end of man is not happiness, nor health, but holiness. . . . The one thing that matters is whether man will accept the God who will make him holy."

As I pondered the thoughts on that page, these words of faith called forth faith on my part to believe that God wanted something of me. They became part of my life; my inner living space, which had seemed cramped and impossible, suddenly enlarged. I read what my spirit needed to hear. The words gave me direction for life.

I had experienced a language event — an experience with words which brought meaning to my life. Most Christians will recognize the same kind of experience in which the words of truth suddenly open new vistas of understanding of oneself, the world and God. People describe the event by saying "the Word spoke to me," or "the Word became precious to me."

This type of language event may occur between a preacher and congregation, in personal devotional reading or other situations. It is the type of encounter with God's Word which brings hope of salvation to the sin-weary person, courage in time of despair or frustration, strength to continue in the face of unsurmountable obstacles.

Though outward circumstances may seem impossible, the power of the Word of God sets one free to act, to work, to reach out. "The words that I have spoken to you are spirit and are life," said Jesus (Jn. 6:63), and countless Christians testify that this is true.

There is another kind of experience with language which is sometimes confused with the true language event. It is the experience which moves one emotionally to tears or laughter, perhaps to nothing, but the words have no lasting effect. They do not become the compelling force which enlarges one's inner world and moves one to action. After the tears have been dried and the laughter has ended, the blessing is also gone. The event touched only the emotions.

Because more Christians seem to have experiences like the second which make them "feel good all over" for a little while but do little to change their lives, and fewer like the first, the function of language, particularly in public meetings, is much debated. Do words actually have as much power as they are claimed to have? Much of what is said in a church service is but a repetition of what was said before. Can such words remain forever meaningful? If one's whole life is committed to God and his service, must words always be in evidence to indicate this attitude? Must prayer always be expressed in words? Why not leave it at the level of attitude?

The general feeling becomes "Let's dispense with words because so little comes of pious phrases." Action is what counts.

I was reminded of this trend to discount words as I attended a large state university graduation recently. What was being said from behind the podium seemed the least significant that afternoon. The audience was more concerned with recording the event in pictures for posterity. As the hundreds of graduates crossed the stage, family members with cameras cocked wandered back and forth towards the front until I thought I was in a circus. The words being intoned over the loudspeaker were only sounds without meaning. No one seemed to be listening.

So some people ask, "Why not dispense with formal graduations? The many words are meaningless." In church services, the echo of these words is "Let's not have so much word-making. They're not getting us anywhere. We've heard them all before."

Elton Trueblood suggests in *A Place to Stand* that Christians need to get more tough-minded in matters of belief. "If God is not, then the sooner we find it out the better. If belief in God is not true, it is an evil and should be eliminated from our entire universe of discourse. If prayer is not an objective encounter with the living God, we shall do well to make this discovery and give up the nonsense as soon as possible."

I would add to his words that if the Bible is not God's Word, and if he doesn't use it and the language of faith to reach people, then let's forget about the making of words. If this is not the case, let's find out why words that should be directive and inspiring have become oppressive and binding. God has promised his Word shall not return to him void. It may be our words that are causing the trouble.

Purr words
and snarl words

33

Katie: *The speaker tonight should never have used the word "community."*

You: *Why not?*

Katie: *There were a few people sitting near the back who think "community" means community of goods. They think this teaching was intended for a people waiting for the second coming, not for people waiting for the architect to show up with plans for their new home.*

You: *Well, would the word "household" have been better?*

Katie: *I don't think so. That still has the connotation of sharing too much of themselves and their goods.*

The neighbor's cat enjoys sunning herself on my patio. She purrs contentedly when I pat her. At the approach of a dog, her back arches, her hair stands on end, probably her blood pressure increases — and she snarls.

Most people are too dignified to purr and snarl, but they do it anyway — with words. Semanticist S.I. Hayakawa says some people might just as well snarl or purr instead of using words. The effect is the same. When a person says "We had a wonderful time," or "That guy is a rat," he or she is not conveying any facts, only a judgment or feeling. The words are a snarl or a purr.

Some people also snarl or purr when they hear certain

words or ideas expressed. Test your friends by reading them a list of words with strong connotations. Have them write a plus for a word which makes them feel like purring and minus for a word which elicits a snarl. Try this list: born-again believer, blood of the Lamb, charismatic, Bible-believing Christian, households, community, evangelism, Bill Gothard, commune, social action, Holy Spirit, missions, Marabel Morgan, social justice, house churches. Now compare answers.

Why, for example, do some people get uptight when a word like community is introduced? The Apostle John (1 Jn. 1:3 *NEB*) writes about believers sharing a common life with the Father and his son Jesus Christ. Yet community and common life sound too much like communism for some, so they snarl.

Another word which gets unpleasant sounds from some people is house church. I'm not sure why, but it seems to connote some kind of subversive activity bound to crumble the foundations of the church institution. Yet the early church frequently met in house churches.

Another snarl word is social justice. Basically it means that the body of Christ works toward ridding social structures of their sin to achieve justice or "honorable relations" for all oppressed. Taking care of the poor and oppressed is a much-mentioned theme in both the Old and New Testaments, but social justice which means helping blacks get a better education doesn't seem to mean the same as when the Apostle Paul was instructed to keep the poor in mind when he took the gospel to the Gentiles (Gal. 2:10). Further, social justice has one word in common with social gospel, a taboo word. Yet most Christians enjoy church socials and socializing. It does get confusing, doesn't it?

What triggers a snarl? What sets off a purr? I think it is a learned reaction, and not instinctive, as for a cat. Many of us middle-aged persons were nurtured on a theology that said Christianity means a personal relationship with God through his son Jesus Christ. Few people would dispute that even today. I don't. That salvation makes the sinner a member of the body of Christ and brings him or her into a continuing relationship with other Christians was a truth never repressed in the past. It was not stressed, because it didn't have to be. A new Christian was expected to join other Christians and not hold back.

Today when extreme self-autonomy ("You are the sole determiner of your life and responsible to no one else") is strongly advocated, the teaching of body life (In Christ, I need you and you need me; we are responsible to and for each other) must be retaught. But community and body life seem like a wrong teaching to some, because these words weren't one of the preacher's three main points three decades ago.

As I see it, the matter of social justice is closely related to the foregoing. Some persons resist the idea that the church get involved in any kind of action to achieve social justice because they think the main work of the church is proclamation — not caring. If enough persons in government were won to Christ, these leaders would change the sinful systems.

This concept sounds good, but if the blacks had waited for the church to convert enough slave owners and legislators to achieve what freedom they now have they would still be using washrooms and drinking fountains marked "Colored."

John Perkins in *The Quiet Revolution* offers a strong argument in support of evangelistic efforts accompanied by efforts for social justice. He started as an evangelist in the South among his own black people, but soon discovered that the gospel was ineffective among people caught in the cycle of poverty. He found it hard to preach about a God of love and mercy to hungry, shivering persons without jobs. So, while maintaining his Bible teaching program, he initiated programs which would give blacks more economic power.

Perkins concludes that when sin organizes itself into structures and systems, as in the case of economic oppression of blacks and poor whites, the corporate body of Christ must fight it. Sin must be found in all forms. The church exists to give the gospel greater power. It must take a corporate stand against corporate sins like poor housing, discrimination, social violence and so forth.

That cat on my patio can't talk. It can only purr or snarl. But people can think and talk. They can move beyond animal sounds to constructive discussions about matters that distress them. So, what makes you snarl? What makes you purr? A letter to the editor of your denominational organ is a good way to start a discussion, especially if it comes without animal sounds.

The book
you never read

34

Katie: *She borrowed the book about three weeks ago. I figured she'd be through with it now, so I asked her how she was enjoying it.*

You: *What'd she say?*

Katie: *Hadn't even started it yet! She planned to read it through this summer — sort of a summer project.*

You: *One book per summer. Sounds like dieting —*

Katie: *Yeah, keep the mind slim but not trim.*

Reading is no longer the favorite pastime of numerous adults, nor will it be of youngsters who must struggle to make it through a book. No doubt some people steer away from current novels because many are unadulterated trash, presenting a debased view of humankind, and with no redeeming social value. The growing popularity of movies has no doubt also had an effect on reading time, as have television and spectator sports.

Yet despite the adverse influences on reading, I believe the church must constantly assert its respect for the power of words and the Word. If it no longer believes that reading changes and shapes the inner being, who will? If the church doesn't confess that reading gives a person strength and courage as well as knowledge and wisdom, the books stored on our shelves at home and in libraries will be lost by default. As

Ray Bradbury points out in *Fahrenheit 451*, a classic science fantasy about a future bookless society, an unread book might as well be a burned book.

In the society he presents, people have quit reading of their own accord because it does not bring them fun and happiness. The development of the inner person has become a worn-out tradition. All citizens of this society are supplied with every technological device to make them blissful. The living room of a home may be equipped with a floor-to-ceiling television screen for each wall. People are kept from thinking seriously by being drowned night and day in music and cacophony heard through small ear receivers.

All magazines have become a "nice blend of vanilla tapioca" and only comic-books and three-dimensional sex magazines have survived. Newspapers have died out like huge moths because no one wants them and no one misses them. People only want to read about "passionate lips and the fist in the stomach."

Schools have become places in which children are crammed full of facts by film-teachers. "School is shortened, discipline relaxed, philosophies, histories, languages dropped, English and spelling gradually neglected, finally almost completely ignored." The schools turn out "runners, jumpers, racers, tinkerers, grabbers, snatchers, fliers and swimmers instead of examiners, critics, knowers and imaginative creators." The word "intellectual" becomes a swear word in this society without books.

A human being has no worth and is run down by young people in cars as a road sport if found walking on the road. "The philosophy governing human behavior seems to be 'Blow your nose on a person, wad them, flush them away, reach for another, blow, wad, flush.'" Life has no responsibilities and no consequences. Conversation has dwindled to cars, clothes and saying, "How swell."

In this society where fun is everything, reading is a legal offense, for it upsets people, especially the minorities. If people read, they think, become concerned and create problems. People who don't read tend to move along with the system and ask no questions.

The job of the fireman in this futuristic society is to burn books rather than to put fires out. If a hidden book is discovered, the entire house is put to the torch by the firemen. Eventually nearly all written materials have been destroyed. Only two Bibles are still known to exist in this part of the world plus a few other important works. And life has become a vast wasteland.

One fireman, Montag, sees his own inner vacuum and the importance of books through the influence of a young girl who still finds joy "in catching the rain in her mouth" and in pondering life. He joins a renegade group of hobo intellectuals with photographic memories who have stored all the great books of all times in their minds so that when the appropriate time comes, they can again be transferred to paper. Their task for the present is simply to remember.

These men recognize that people cannot be forced to read or to see its value. One comments, "You can't make people listen. They have to come round in their own time, wondering what happened and why the world blew up under them." For even when people had books on hand a long time ago they didn't use them.

The time this man is referring to is now. We have books. But do we read them? Bradbury's grim new world seems an impossible reality. But the truth underlying it cannot be denied. It may take some kind of catastrophe to show us that to read is a privilege which can only be retained through use.

Language pollution

35

Katie: *Some people are sure good at it —*
You: *At what?*
Katie: *Using words as a cover-up. I didn't understand one word that was said at that meeting, yet I came away feeling we must have the world's greatest program for the systematic relief of upset fishermen.*
You: *What happened?*
Katie: *The words kept coming, but I couldn't find one I could pin down long enough to discover its meaning.*

Every weekend I am irresistibly drawn to the sports pages. I have this irrational desire to see by what new ingenious method Team A beat Team B. Team A does not merely defeat Team B. They mop, bomb, gong, clobber, grind, maul and even skunk. If the margin of winning isn't large, they only mug, wax, rob, lop, exit or conk the other team. If the game is close, they edge, nip, clip, topple or skim the loser.

As I devour these headlines, I almost forget to notice scores or even who played. If a person from outerspace read the sports pages, I'm sure he'd think an athletic event was a savage frenzy in which players grind and rip each other into shreds.

Words are funny things. They can be bent in any direction to create an effect or an image which doesn't necessarily match the real thing. In the case of basketball, the sportswriters want to make the game sound more exciting, so they make it sound more vicious. If they keep at it, the game may eventually fulfill their prophetic words.

But this bending of words isn't unique to sportswriting. We live in a society determined not to tell the truth, whether in business, politics, charities or even religion. There is a growing trend to use words to sell an image of a product or person instead of the objective reality. Our language is full of euphemisms (expressions designed to make reality more tolerable), jargon and doublespeak. Some euphemisms are harmless. If talking about death as "passing away" helps some people, most of us don't mind. The problem is compounded, however, when jargon and euphemisms are used to deliberately destroy and deceive.

Advertisers are prime deceivers, using euphemisms to compel the buyer to rush to the store to buy their product. A used Cadillac is billed as "young, beautiful, with a little experience," and a second-hand Volkswagen is listed as "pre-owned." Credit terms are always "reasonable" or "convenient," but the ads don't say for whom. A real estate person always sells a "home," not a house, and the insurance agents sell a "homeowner's policy." Liquor ads sell a way of life that is carefree, joyous and fulfilling, never mentioning the agony and pain that may accompany the purchase.

Television viewers know that commercials take much stamina to watch. Their producers use rhetorical overkill, describing things as greater or worse than they are. Advertisers, of course, describe their products as bigger and better. They employ witless women to sing the praises of soap, deodorant, toothpaste and peanut butter with the abandon of one who has at long last found eternal salvation for her family. Apparently listeners believe what they hear, or else the advertisers wouldn't continue their trench warfare in our family rooms.

In educational circles terms like "dean" and "vice-president," which once enjoyed clearly defined meanings, have been inflated as much as the budgets of their schools, spawning new deans and vice-presidents all over university campuses with the profligacy of caged rabbits.

Proposal writers, whose tribe is increasing daily, state they are aware of their doublespeak, or lack of preciseness in language, yet feel compelled to use it to keep programs going and funds flowing their way.

Some professions build and defend themselves by a selective language. To speak in psychiatric or sociological jargon like "complementary role expectation sanction systems" allows a person to give the impression of being a professional without being one.

What about the church? Have its spokespersons also adopted the techniques and language of Madison Avenue to sell an image or to stay ahead of the rat race? Do the people of the church, like advertisers, push language to its extremes, so that it can't bear the load of meaning it is supposed to convey?

The answer is yes if we are convinced that commercial advertising methods are the best methods to promote what the church stands for. "A challenging and inspiring message awaits you at First Happiness Church," states the four-color bulletin. When a pewsitter has read those words for ten years or more, knowing that some services were good, others quite ordinary, and a few challenging and inspiring as prophesied, is it any wonder the words "challenging and inspiring" no longer are meaningful? The image and the real thing don't agree any more than the commercial about the housewife who has discovered laundry joy begins with Brand X.

The answer is yes if we believe the church cannot be persuasive in promoting the gospel without gimmickry, jargon and linguistic overkill: "the nation's most outstanding Bible preacher," "mission orientation dialogue," "evaluation study teams," or "Tonight you will hear the truth for the first time about what God has to say about the Middle East."

The answer is yes if we no longer trust language to communicate clearly and feel pressured to disguise facts behind a shelter of abstractions. George Orwell's classic Newspeak has been translated into church terms as Churchspeak. Simply stated it means wrenching a word from its reality in the objective world and making it sound like more than it actually is.

An example that comes to mind is the way some leaders push causes under the umbrella-word, "the Lord's work" to gain support from the sincere congregation for an actual need to keep a mission hospital going or to replace the outdated, but not outworn, rug in the fellowship hall. If a leader can get the people to call any cause the Lord's work, the battle is won. Such an appeal always appears valid and cannot be disputed.

One young person told me the language of some church professionals sounds like "words coming from another world." At times I agree, especially when I have to translate their abstract, cotton-wool expressions into what I think they mean. The words create an aura of pomposity and erudition, but are actually puffery and fluffery.

Morality begins with language. Word and act are inseparable. They must agree or words soon lose their currency and become mere tokens of exchange.

The
p.r. mentality

36

Katie: *But what he said during that meeting isn't even close to the truth. He said the situation looked good, very good — and I know from talking to the persons involved that the situation looks far from good — even bad. How could he say such a thing?*

You: *If he says it the way it is, some people may get upset about this project and not contribute another cent. Some immature Christians can't handle the truth, so they have to be fed a watered-down version to keep them giving.*

Katie: *But is money and popularity more important than truth-speaking?*

You: *It isn't really dishonest — it's simply that one's reach should exceed one's grasp. You don't talk publicly about the grasp — only about the reaching.*

Like most people, I found myself sorting out some of the events of Watergate leading to President Nixon's resignation. I struggled to fit together the image the public had of Nixon as a pious, moral, sincere, earnest individual, working for the good of the people, and the image which grew clearer after the tapes were revealed. Then the public saw him as a man more interested in personal power than the people's welfare. He seemed to work from an amoral framework, using lies when they suited his purposes and stumbling into the gutter with his private language as soon as he was out of the public eye.

What happened?

In a *Time* interview, in referring to another White House figure, the writer said, "He seems caught up in the White House philosophy that everything can be handled in a p.r. context."

The p.r. context. That seems to be it. Or at least part of the answer.

This public relations mentality which characterized Nixon and the White House is common to many institutions dependent upon public opinion for their support. In its extreme forms, it requires that public opinion be kept favorable by any and all means, fair or foul. Rigging or manipulating information, screening out unfavorable facts which might blotch the image, is acceptable behavior. Nixon was not alone in believing that p.r. can clear away any obstruction.

Consider the now defunct World Football League. When it first began operation it appeared to have overwhelming success in drawing fans. It pointed to the huge paying crowds at its first two nationally televised games. Later the truth about gate receipts leaked out. Five of the 21 World Football League teams had given away 158,000 free tickets to their home games. Paid attendance at the league's first 24 games averaged 24,000 a game. The Philadelphia officials admitted wholesale lying, saying that more than 100,000 of the team's 120,253 spectators at its first two games entered free. Figures for other games were equally misleading.

"We just had to do it or we would have been a joke," said the vice-president.

Because commercial advertising and public relations works so well, church institutions are sometimes sucked into manipulative uses of language also, writes James E. Sellers in *The Outsider and the Word of God: A Study in Christian Communication*. He identifies several dangers, while acknowledging that because the church manifests itself in society as an institution, we must be willing to accept publicizing as one of the necessary modes of communication for the church.

The concern of a public relations expert is to present a positive image of the institution to the public. Sellers points out this goal may tend to make the publicity arm of the church institution get its theology a little lopsided. "It tends to view the church as a fellowship of worthies rather than as a corporation of sinners." The news sent out is only about the good and successful things about the inner workings of the institution. He says this approach may provide some background "static" which interferes with the proclamation of the gospel, for the gospel is for sinners and public relations is only about saints.

Such publicity gives an incomplete picture of the institution by leaving out unpleasant information. It works on the assumption that the ordinary pewsitter cannot handle difficult information about the church-related school, mission or relief organization, and that his or her support will weaken when he or she finds out coworkers at another level are human.

Sellers sees a second danger in that the church institution may come to depend on "communication as a matter of good techniques of self-promotion." Any good deed, any exhibition of virtue such as honesty and self-sacrifice or helpfulness, is often not felt to be "validated" until it receives its due share of publicity. Someone must get credit for good actions done.

He sees a third problem in the way public relations people must fight to control their world like their equivalents in the secular world. The issues become a matter of striving for control and power to get their share of the financial pie or available dollars, which puts the church out of its proper sphere entirely. "When the church takes publicity as a model for all of its communications, we may be sure that it disenables itself from presenting itself to the world as a suffering servant or from commending self-sacrifice as a dominant Christian motif."

I read that, then sit back to say, "Oh, come now, Sellers, that couldn't happen in the church! Leaving out pertinent information to keep the image bright and shining, the use of oversell, slanting information, gobbledygook — the tools of the persuasive writer — are not found in the land of the church-person.''

Well, perhaps not intentionally, but anything that works as well as mass advertising has its temptations. Although understanding, trust and belief are the true goals of the p.r. person, the fear of losing credibility is sometimes so great, some persons in charge of the public image are tempted to make slight, very slight, distortions or misrepresentations of facts for competitive advantage.

The ball park figure of persons who attended a function is rounded out generously. The story of the gift of a donor is framed in such words, which while not inaccurate, do not clarify to an unsuspecting reader what the fine print contained. And any story with a negative connotation is withdrawn entirely, as if it had never happened. Can common people actually not handle the truth about such matters and about failures and problems in church-related institutions if given adequate information? What I hear is that some facts have to be presorted, pretreated for stains, washed in the gentle cycle and tumble-dried for the immature who shut their pocketbooks or quit subscribing and attending when they hear unpleasant news or news which doesn't agree with their thinking. So like quick-sand, the p.r. mentality slowly sucks the unwilling journalist into its mire. Survival on the job and of the institution is at stake. Why quibble?

The basic issue, as I see it, is whether the supporting constituency is entitled to the whole truth about all matters, not merely a laundered version which reads well. Most often, what is controversial in the church is not outright fraud or corruption or embezzlement of funds, but a matter of waste — an over-whelming duplication of time, energy and money — and divi-siveness and rigidity. Is the constituency being treated fairly and in a Christian manner when bad news is buried in the files? Can the constituency be taught to give trust if credibility is not established over a period of time?

As a Christian writer I struggle with the question of

honesty about difficult issues all the time — especially those close to home. The events that happen in Washington or Florida are easier to pontificate about. How open and forthright can I write and still hang onto readers? To write about controversy is controversial, so when I find myself edging close to a sensitive issue, do I toss out my true — but false — start and begin again on a more benign subject?

I can see where today's p.r. agent would have suffered a heart attack in New Testament times at what was allowed to pass into biblical history. Today we know that many people turned back after Jesus mixed socially with publicans and prostitutes (hardly good for the image, as some public figures today can attest), that Paul had a stiff argument with Barnabas, and that on another occasion he withstood Peter to the face. And certainly, a report of the ignominious defeat of the cross would have been ruled out by the p.r. person concerned with keeping Christ's public image intact.

Through words and deeds Christ taught vulnerability before the world. A Christian institution which operates within a p.r. context protects itself by its own power structures from any form of vulnerability — or from crucifixion. And dies that way also.

As I reread the stories of Christ, Paul and the other early New Testament leaders, the positive impressions of these personalities are strengthened as I am made aware of how the grace of God worked with human weakness.

A church caught in a mass media syndrome which promotes success tends to forget that failure can become a learning experience. Failure brings people together as much as success, if treated in the right manner. If we omit the pain and the struggle of our corporate pilgrimage, we no longer show the church as a group of sinners for whom grace and judgment are real. When the picture is always pleasant, Christ becomes another beautifully packaged commodity, like detergent or deodorant. And we buyers find ourselves working to get rid of rings around the collar and bathtub instead of around the heart.

*. . . about
the will
to be one*

The
sharing game

37

Katie: *I hate going to meetings where we form small groups and then the leader says brightly, "Share!" What if I have nothing to share?*

You: *A Christian always has something to share—*

Katie: *Not this one. Sometimes I feel pretty dry — dryer than my front lawn in August.*

You: *Wouldn't that be something you could share honestly — your feeling of emptiness?*

The pewsitters were numbered off, and the resultant groups told to form small circles and to "share."

Share? Share what?

I stumble at the word which has arrived only lately in our evangelical vocabulary, and which the young use euphemistically for anything related to Christian activity.

What should we share? What should we give each other? A few empty words? A part of our lives? A few uncomfortable moments of time? How does one share with others when one has never been taught how to perform this activity except in a formal testimony meeting?

Further, before one can share, one must have something to distribute. Years ago, when Mother told us to share the candy Father had brought home, I knew perfectly well she meant handing some of the jelly beans to each brother and sister. But in Christian terminology, "share" has become an orphaned verb, deprived of its object. People just "share," and it's not always clear what they're handing out.

Can one share one's faith with people one knows and yet doesn't know? Can one share freely in a small circle, as one looks into the faces of people one has come to recognize only by the backs of their coat collars and hair styles?

And so we sat there for a while . . . the silence dropping heavily between our chairs . . . waiting for the sharing to take place . . . waiting for the one with the largest amount of faith to give some to the rest of us.

A cautious groping for amiability came first.

"Is this all who's going to be in our group?"

"We're sure a varied bunch."

"Anyone have something to say first?"

"Where did you say you grew up? She was your mother? Oh, yes . . . I think I knew her when she was a girl. . . ."

And then a scurrying into the dim recesses of the mind to find an experience, any experience that might be deemed suitable, before silence — the prickly kind — reached around each person to cover him or her as with a heavy wool blanket on a warm, humid night.

"Surely someone has had some kind of an experience with the Lord this week? Something you read or someone you talked to . . . ?"

What was that passage I read in the Bible last Thursday? Somehow I know it fitted into what I was doing at the time. Why didn't I bring my Bible along this evening?

What a longing for words, suitable words, spiritual words, to fill the verbal void. *Why can't anyone think of something to say so our group won't seem so ignorant? Some of the other groups are doing a lot of talking. If this were a testimony meeting, one could quote a Scripture verse, but here it seems out of place . . . too much like filler.*

The day's experiences close in — the busyness, the memory of an encounter with a neighbor and the ensuing misunderstanding, the plans which need to be made for the summer . . . milk must be bought on the way home . . . *I think I forgot to empty the dryer. . . .*

Why am I so quiet? Why is Elise withdrawn tonight? She hasn't said a word all evening. How can I learn to know her, this person placed beside me, with whom I am to share the inner condition of my Christian life? Can I open my life to her and hope for new meanings and relationships? Maybe I should just tell them what I said at the mission circle meeting the other night about how God has promised to answer our prayers. Maybe that'll get someone started to share. . . .

And then the quiet one at the far side said in a small, half-troubled voice, cutting through the tangle of wayward words and mired thoughts, "I don't know how to share," and welcomed us into her life.

Which is where we should have all started.

Room for grace

38

Katie: *I hate myself for not having said anything — for having let him run right over me with his steamroller words and push me flat to the ground.*

You: *But Christ says to be submissive — to be the servant of all.*

Katie: *But does that mean I let people walk over me? They may be walking over my prone body, but I'm standing straight up inside.*

You: *At the moment when aggression most abounds, grace can also abound.*

Katie: *I wonder.*

I admit to having problems reconciling our society's emphasis on individualism, self-assertiveness and self-realization with Christ's words, "If any man will come after me, let him deny himself" (Mt. 16:24).

One voice says loudly, "Learn to protect yourself. Don't let yourself get caught in a situation in which others can take advantage of you. If involved in decision-making, become objective. Calculate the risks. Never assume the other person will look after your needs. Always consider how any spontaneous gesture of softness or support of a weaker person may hurt your image." The message is "Survive at all costs. Build people-proof walls around yourself."

The words of Christ, on the other hand, spell vulnerability, dependence upon others, sacrifice and risk-taking. They assure that if you leave your right to yourself behind, the true nature of your personality will emerge and wholeness result.

Can both positions be right?

I admit that most Christians need greater boldness in being and doing for Christ. At times, when the opportunity arrives to give that great testimony, faith shrinks to the size of a lapel cross and words are even more timid. Would a course in self-assertiveness remedy this need?

I agree also that many Christians need help in seeing themselves as worthwhile and lovable persons. Who hasn't come across a Sorrowful Sadie or a Sighing Sam who hate themselves and don't know that lack of self-esteem is their problem? They need to see themselves as "OK" persons. The goals of some self-improvement courses are to help such persons take more effective control of their lives and stand up to the pressures which push them face down into the muck of life.

Yet as I look over the vast numbers of "how-to" books available, I feel we are being pressured into becoming amateur psychologists: read a few books, listen to a few cassettes, attend a workshop or two, tinker with the problem areas of life, and everything will once again be like Sunday dinner at Mother's where the gravy boat never ran dry. The cure of the soul is instant and sure.

I watch these emphases infiltrating the church and its institutions. They look good and necessary. We need to learn to love ourselves, to confront one another and to live more harmoniously.

Then I think of another way which looked just as good when it first began. Most of us who are now middle-aged and older helped usher it in and bring it over the top. At the beginning, it seemed to assure the progress and success of the church as a body. Yet the end result was its institutionalization.

The emphasis began with introducing better techniques for doing church work. Were they needed? Of course. Sunday

schools, youth groups, children's activities, midweek services
— all church programs were streamlined. Budgets were unified
and enlarged. I could go on and on, but as I look back on that
growing trend to rely on human resources, something important got shoved out. *Koinonia* or body life had no room to grow.
It was replaced by a strong chauvinistic loyalty to buildings
and programs. We worshiped God, but found our organizations
could get along without him. They could thrive with strong
doses of human enthusiasm and effort.

What will get edged out if today's human potential movements get lopsided? Possibly room for the Spirit to reveal the
grace of God. We may no longer need works of grace in the
human heart.

The Apostle Paul assured his followers at Ephesus, Corinth
and Philippi that the grace of God would be sufficient for them
at all times. It would be sufficient when they were insufficient.
It would be sufficient when they felt pummelled, pushed and
taken advantage of. It would be sufficient when they were sick,
distressed and lacked wisdom. It would provide light, strength
and joy when circumstances denied these should be present.
God's grace provided help when human resources failed.

Flannery O'Connor, a Southern writer whose works are
growing in importance, wrote much about the grace of God. She
was able to capture in her stories a glimpse of that brief
moment when the light of God's grace breaks through, offering
opportunity for redemption. In "The Artificial Nigger," a
proud old man, determined to teach his uppity grandson a
lesson, takes him to the big city. They wander around. Both get
lost. The grandfather denies his grandson three times. The boy
rejects his elder. Then before an ancient statue of a Negro, they
recognize the mystery of God's grace. It dissolves their differences like an act of mercy. The grandfather stands "appalled,
judging himself with the thoroughness of God, while the action
of mercy covered his pride like a flame and consumed it. . . . He
realized that he was forgiven for sins from the beginning of
time. . . . He saw that no sin was too monstrous for him to claim

as his own, and since God loved in proportion as He forgave, he felt ready at that instant to enter Paradise." The old man burns with shame because he has so little of this grace to take home with him.

A lesson: Where diplomacy, common sense and self-protectiveness most abound, God's grace can abound in greater measure.

Crossing the line

39

> **You:** *Why'd you agree to be nominated for that committee?*
>
> **Katie:** *But it represents an opportunity to do something for the Lord.*
>
> **You:** *Like so much! It means you'll make yourself so busy running to some committee meetings you won't have time for anything else. You know you're a hog for work.*
>
> **Katie:** *No, I'm not. I just like being involved.*
>
> **You:** *Involved in what?*
>
> **Katie:** *How can I know when I overdo something? Do you get spiritual indigestion?*
>
> **You:** *I think you'll know.*

As children we played a game called prisoner's base. I'm not sure what the rules of the game were, but an imaginary line divided our playing field. If we stood on our side of the line, we were home free; if we crossed the line and someone tagged us, we became their prisoner.

Much of life is similar to that game. A thin invisible line divides many areas of life. On one side is freedom and joy; on the other, slavery and despair.

For example, eating is a wholesome necessary activity. Human beings must eat to live. Yet at some point some people cross the thin line and become prisoners of their eating habits.

Eating becomes gluttony. Something good becomes harmful. Yet where is the dividing line? At two potato chips or three?

But, then, overeating is not your problem. So let's move on.

Righteous anger is justified in the Scriptures. "Be angry and sin not," wrote the Apostle Paul to the Ephesians. It's okay to get angry, but not to let that anger turn to sin. At times I think our churches have too few angry people — persons who are disturbed enough about organized crime, drug pushers, political corruption, hate organizations like the Ku Klux Klan and other forms of prejudice and injustice, to do something about it. On the other hand, we have too many angry people who take out their hostilities on the first person handy. Christ upset the tables of the moneychangers in his righteous anger. We tend to upset breakfast tables and meeting tables.

Zeal to do the Lord's work is good and necessary. We need people with burning zeal, willing to forego all for the sake of the kingdom of God. But who hasn't watched what looked like zeal turn on itself and become lust for power and position? Church servants become workaholics, their families and God left far behind as they push up the ladder. Somewhere a very fine line was crossed from that which was God-given and God-directed to that which is ego-driven and decided by self.

God has given human beings the faculty to reason and think logically. Those who have this gift should thank God daily for it. Yet, instead of using their reasoning powers, some people become prisoners of their own rationalizations and encase themselves in a solid cement wall of their opinions. And there they're stuck. I've been there myself. To change one's mind seems like self-betrayal, but when did I cross the line from reason to rationalization?

Self-respect is needed to keep us functioning as whole persons. Yet it, too, can switch to pride easily. The Quakers were known for their modesty, especially in dress. All wore gray clothes in conservative styles. However, among them were wealthy Quakers who went to Paris to find materials of special quality and shade of gray indicative of their wealthy position. This material became known as Quaker linen. Self-respect and humility became pride. The line had been crossed.

In each case, on one side is a legitimate activity or emotion. But then the individual crosses the line and the good emotion turns over and becomes ugly and hurtful to self and others. Love becomes lust, humility becomes pride, zeal becomes power-seeking, assertion becomes aggression, and so forth.

How do we keep from crossing the line? Paul wrote to the Galatians, "If you are led of the Spirit, you will not satisfy the desires of your lower nature" (Gal. 5:16). The Holy Spirit can keep us from crossing the line. But how?

Not through magic, though most of us would appreciate a Gideon's fleece or two to set out occasionally. Not through some strong audible voice saying, "Time to quit gossiping." Not through some invisible hands pushing away second helpings of cherry pie a la mode.

Nor is it a deep dark secret when we cross the line to gluttony, unrighteous anger and selfishness, for Christians have the mind of Christ. "Incredible as it may sound," wrote Paul, "we who are spiritual have the very thoughts of Christ" (1 Cor. 2:16 *Phillips*). An inner knowledge is involved which is not available to non-Christians (v. 14).

To have this knowledge does not demand impulsive decision-making. Someone once said God gives us time to make decisions, but the devil expects us to move in a hurry. One man who spoke harshly against an issue was asked why he hadn't kept quiet. He replied he was afraid the Spirit would caution him against speaking and he would lose his chance to speak his mind.

To know the mind of Christ does not mean never making a mistake. God provides a way for renewal through forgiveness for the times we miss the line. It does require a willingness to listen and to obey. I find my problem in crossing the line usually occurs when I am too tired or too scheduled to listen to

God's voice. When time gets short, what gets knocked out of the schedule first? Quiet time, reflection time, Bible study time. Meals, classes, committee meetings, evening news, all get first priority.

Having the mind of Christ means we can know when we get to the line. But then we have to decide not to cross over.

Minicourses
for living

40

Katie: *What actually changes — the truth of Scripture, the way we conceptualize this truth, or our culture?*

You: *A little of all three?*

Katie: *Hardly, for the Bible doesn't change. Would you agree though that the teachings of faith and life have shifted with the times — once the emphasis was on salvation from hell, now it's on community and social justice. What next?*

You: *I think it's mostly a matter of balancing one against the other. When you push a wall too hard from one side, you have to go to the other side and push it back in line.*

I remember a few occasions during my days as an eighth-grader when a classmate would come to school before the bell rang, gather up his books, wave a half-sheepish, half-triumphant good-bye and leave. This day was his sixteenth birthday. He had attended school for as long as the law required. Now he was a free person.

Those recollections are fully compensated for by the sight of senior citizens trooping back to the classroom each week on college campuses across the nation. Some are well over sixty, some over seventy and a few over eighty. Continuing education for adults is in. No longer do we have to defend the idea that a human being is teachable until death. People are no longer afraid to accept that creativity can be set free at any age, for learning is never a completed activity. In our day, an education is more perishable than a lettuce salad left in the sun on the picnic table.

One educator said recently that rapid change is so permeating every sphere of human activity that we may anticipate beginning compulsory education for the middle-aged and elderly. He was thinking, of course, of updating education for self-development, for vocational and professional competency, for health and welfare, and for civic, political and community involvement.

I can suggest some courses to be included in such an updating curriculum. One friend suggested that every individual should take a course in how to make friends. He was not interested in courses in psychology or sociology, he said, but in learning to trust another person, to forgive, and especially to find the courage to risk dialogue and confrontation. Too many people move into old age without these skills. They have been taught to function defensively, guarding themselves against exploitation and manipulation by others.

Another course for late bloomers might be learning to listen. Although more than a decade has passed since civil rights headlined the news, black spokespersons still keep telling us, 'We hurt when you leave us out, or when you reveal by your attitudes and actions we don't belong." The white society, including the church, has been told this hundreds of times. Yet those speakers have to keep reminding us — some seriously, some humorously, some with pathos, others with bitterness, hoping we will catch on.

They aren't the only ones pleading, "Listen to me." Recently an older minister commented that "retired minister" meant "useless minister." He was hurting, because he had been put aside, when he still felt he had something to offer. But no one was listening.

Some singles, whether never-married, divorced or widowed, dare to whisper similar words. One single woman said, "When I think about church, I could cry." She was tired of trying to fit into a congregation which didn't know what to do with her. But no one heard her cry of pain. So listening would be a good course for those of us who are growing older.

I'd like to add another course to this special curriculum for those moving along in years, a course on how to cope with change, particularly theological change. I sense the church has many puzzled people who cannot understand the changes in the theological world. They are floundering, greatly troubled because the package of theological learning they wrapped up and tied carefully twenty or more years ago no longer is adequate. Middle-aged and older people became familiar and comfortable with one theology — a theology of salvation, missions and evangelism, stewardship and church loyalty. Today they are confronted with and are expected to understand liberation theology, relational theology, black theology, process theology and several more.

Bewildered and uneasy by the urges to keep up with the times, the elderly become defensive and resentful as they counter the challenge to liberalize their beliefs. Every spokesperson for change, and especially those with long, straggly prophet beards and haircuts become the enemy. That another definition of discipleship might be possible escapes them. They want only the security of the old.

When you've got persons who cling to the old theology and those who are open proponents of some of the current theologies, a type of polarization is certain to take place. The latter group, increasingly at ease with their new freedom, become arrogant and contemptuous of those who cannot see the Christian life as they do and who aren't overwhelmed by the new emphases. The others are baffled and angry.

This taking of sides is inevitable because the two groups live in two different theological worlds. Each group's concept of God differs according to the tradition in which its members were taught — with the usual amount of human perversion thrown in. If older people are hostile or indifferent to change, they are consistent with what they have learned about God —

a God who changes not cannot be in favor of change. Change and decay belong together, not change and progress.

Anthropologist Margaret Mead writes that in our society the young are the natives and the old the foreigners. The young were born and raised in a technological society. The old began their lives in another era. In the church, the young are growing up with a theology of relevance and involvement, while the old are still living with a theology which emphasizes primarily a vertical relationship with God. So I think we need a lifetime course in understanding change, and if necessary, to unlearn old concepts.

But I can't omit one last course. I suggest it be one which lets all Christians know Satan has not yet retired on his dubious social security benefits. I sense how unprepared we are for the experience of the demonic, not only in ourselves and other Christians, but especially in the church and its agencies and institutions. We expect Satan to work in society at large, at the porno places and beer halls, but not where we believe Christ is Lord. We are not prepared for the destructive attacks of the enemy, and hesitate to believe he may be sitting in at some committee session, even though it may have begun with prayer. We need lessons in recognizing sin and evil.

Is this a worthwhile curriculum? It was part of the curriculum Christ used with his disciples. He warned Peter to guard against Satan's attacks. He taught his disciples to love their neighbor as themselves. He gave them the example of the Good Samaritan who felt a stranger's pain as his own.

Our responsibilities, legal or moral, to this curriculum are never fulfilled at any age — sixteen or sixty. This kind of learning continues for a lifetime.

The church
we're building

41

Katie: *When you think of church what comes to mind?*

You: *I wish it wasn't a building, but it is. I hear the word church and I think of a structure — bricks and mortar and pews — and its street address.*

Katie: *Will it always be like this? Was it always like this? Will the visible structure ever be less important again than the people who are the body of Christ?*

Inflation. The energy crisis. The Middle East stalemate. These problems have preempted the attention given to the struggles of the church to break the bonds of institutionalization. Only rarely does the issue hit the newspapers anymore.

Apparently those who didn't like what was happening have spun off into experimental groups, like the Jesus people or small-group movement, and are doing their thing alone. Others have dropped out altogether, finding the general upheaval about the church an opportune moment to ease out of what they never felt a part of.

Some have decided to begin rebuilding the church from within, and others, who always liked the church exactly the way it was, still haven't figured out what all the shouting was about.

What was the shouting about? Should we let the issue subside? The key question seems to be what constitutes the church? What did Christ intend when he spoke of building his church? Brick and mortar or human lives?

Because decades of tradition easily and firmly mold our concepts of the church, try a short quiz to help you see where your thinking is taking you.

1. When someone says "church," I immediately think of (a) a building; (b) a mainline denomination; (c) a conference; (d) an ethnic or cultural group; (e) a unique community of believers; (f) none of the above; (g) all of the above.

2. I believe the following qualifications must be met before I consider a group of believers a full-fledged church: (a) has an official membership role; (b) is fully self-supporting, not a "mission"; (c) affiliated with a denomination; (d) conducts a graded Sunday school; (e) no longer meets in a home, hall or other temporary facility; (f) operates with a full schedule of weekly services; (g) none of these.

3. The site for our meetinghouse was chosen because of (a) tradition (it's always been there); (b) economic reasons; (c) respectability of neighborhood; (d) convenience of people who attend; (e) possibilities for expansion; (f) nearness to people without a church home; (g) none of the above.

4. The type of architecture of our sanctuary (structure, windows, steeple, arches, etc.) was determined by (a) economic reasons; (b) aesthetic values; (c) tastes and standards of living of the building committee; (d) fashion in church architecture; (e) worship aids.

5. The arrangement of church pews (bolted down, padded, straight rows, facing the front, circular) has been maintained because it is (a) the most efficient arrangement for the janitor; (b) the way most churches do it; (c) the best way for the preacher to hold the attention of the congregation; (d) more orderly than loose chairs; (e) the congregation expects it; (f) all of these.

6. The number and nature of other facilities (kitchen, education wing, committee rooms, fellowship halls, etc.) were chosen (a) for creature comfort; (b) to aid outreach to delin-

quents, addicts, young people, old people; (c) to match the servant character of the church.

7. The present pattern of the Sunday morning service is maintained (a) because of tradition; (b) to keep the regulars coming; (c) to give people time to watch the electronic church first; (d) to promote an atmosphere of openness and worship.

8. The purpose of the organ prelude is (a) to kill time before the service starts; (b) to muffle the noise of people whispering; (c) to give the choir a few minutes to practice; (d) to keep in step with current music fashions; (e) to aid silent worship.

Some modern prophets believe the church of the 21st century will be a church without walls. Little will be visible to the casual observer — no paved parking lots, no steeples, no stained-glass windows — but the worshiper will experience more the power and presence of the Spirit. What will the church of the future be like according to the way you answered this quiz?

Am I my brother's keeper?

42

Katie: — *but I've always been taught that being a missionary is just about the highest calling. Now you're telling me it might be different.*

You: *Well, not exactly — but times have changed and there are other kinds of service opportunities —*

Katie: *That's always the answer —* **times have changed.** *Does that mean truth changes also? Doesn't God's Word remain the same?*

You: *It does, but —*

"Am I my brother's keeper?" asked the speaker, a prominent church leader from India, of his totally white audience.

"Yup," I nodded, as I inwardly marshalled arguments in support of my answer: The Bible says so; didn't God tell Cain he was Abel's keeper. . . ?

"No," continued the speaker, "a Christian is not his brother's keeper." My head shot up. I sat upright. He was disturbing the staid waters of biblical teaching regarding missions. Not my brother's keeper? Haven't several generations of Christians grown up believing themselves to be the keepers of the souls of their benighted brothers and sisters in the dark continents of India and Africa?

"Cain asked this question of God," the speaker explained, "yet God's answer shows that it was not a valid question. A Christian is not his brother's keeper, but his brother's brother.

A keeper is one who holds the keys and the moneybag; he holds power and dispenses authority. The Indian Christians don't want you as their keeper; they want you as their brother."

He's changing the curriculum regarding missions, I mumbled to myself. That Scripture verse could never again bring me a feeling of security regarding my feelings toward overseas missions.

But he wasn't finished yet. A new curriculum always means a new terminology. Sure enough, out went the traditional term "missionary." "Worn out," he said, "no longer useful." Out went the missionary compound idea. "Also outdated," he indicated, for India with its complex, problem-ridden caste system does not need another caste, even a missionary caste. "Come as a brother or sister, a person — not as a missionary," he concluded.

Although his ideas about the changing face of missions were not new, hearing them from a national leader gave the words new import. "This is final," he seemed to say. "Missions overseas has changed. Get with it."

As I looked over the congregation, many of whom were middle-aged or older, I wondered, "Can the over-forty group change to this new course of study? How easy is it to forget the old missions festivals when the sanctuary, packed from front to back with faithful supporters, shook to the words of "There's a call comes ringing o'er the restless waves, Send the light"? How quickly can one erase the memory of the impact of the missionary message which opened one's pocketbook like nothing had before? How can one empty oneself of concepts which have nourished one's spiritual life for decades?

Summed up, the old curriculum of the church interpreted the cross of Christ in simple terms of "Go, give and pray." The most important verse in the New Testament was the "Go ye" verse, and to go to the farthest parts of the world because we were keepers had the most merit. If one couldn't go, one could give to the Lord's work (and to give to missions overseas always seemed to have more worth than paying the janitor's salary or the light bill). If one couldn't go or give, one could always pray. Important as prayer was, for some it was a way out of the rest of the mandate.

The old curriculum for missions had a spot for everyone, rich or poor, strong or weak, and enabled many people to build a rich, meaningful life for themselves as they helped to usher in the kingdom of God, even if they couldn't see what was happening close up. Being the keeper of a brother's soul in a faraway land seemed like the essence of Christianity, even if the emphasis in the homeland was on the well-being of the keeper rather than on the one being kept.

Yet I thought I heard the Indian church leader say a radical redefinition of the cross is necessary. Times have changed. Our mission theology must also change from a keeper theology to a brother theology. This new way of looking at missions makes room for all Christians at all levels of church life, not just those at the receiving end. A brother not only offers help but is willing to receive it. He doesn't make all the decisions alone, but lets his brother overseas take part in the decision-making process. A brother theology means more than offering a formula for redemption. It means joining forces to find together the answers to peace, injustice, poverty and hunger. It embraces a fellowship of equals.

Can people change? Middle-aged Americans are what they are because they have faithfully followed the curriculum the way it was taught them. Will some now think that all that went before was wasted effort? Will others, with a sense of false pride, cling to the old curriculum, refusing to accept the changes? Will they become more conservative and more bewildered as they see what gave life meaning and purpose slipping from their grasp? Can they come to understand that missions can still happen without terms like "missionary," "compound" and "field," and that it can happen today, here in this country, as well as overseas?

The kind of commitment they gave to the old curriculum is needed now for the "brother" approach.

Footprints in the sands of time

43

Katie: *At times I get so mad I could spit because those who are supposed to be leaders never lead. They simply don't speak up — they only speak after they sense the feeling of the group.*

You: *Well, you know that if a young minister moving up the ecclesiastical ladder were to speak up strongly on something touchy, like women's roles in the church, he'd be labeled a male feminist and probably lose any chance of upward mobility.*

Katie: *So what? Shouldn't one always speak one's convictions?*

You: *I think it depends on whether you're speaking to show your clout or whether you want to strengthen the community of Christ.*

Katie: *And in the meantime, no one says anything . . .*

A popular and principal pastime of followers is to discuss their leaders. If these leaders tick, then the topic is what makes them tick. If they don't, the topic is why the works have broken down. It may also be true the principal pastime of leaders is discussing their followers, but that's another topic.

Along with most institutions, the church is suffering a crisis in leadership. Yet what produces leaders? I wonder why some communities I am familiar with have produced more than their share of church leaders. Were the circumstances so difficult and rigid that only the strong could survive? Or did forceful spiritual leaders evoke others to follow in their footsteps?

Do leaders emerge when a crisis occurs? Or do persons who are leaders direct events so that the church can move ahead? Do the events make the leader or the leader bring about the events? At what point does a person receive the gift of leadership from the Spirit?

The church needs giants again — not the kind the ten spies saw when they checked out the promised land for the Israelites, but men and women who stand head and shoulders above others spiritually and who are able to shout the rallying cry to battle for the kingdom of God in such a way that their followers pick up arms.

Today, the church has many important persons, many extremely capable and well-qualified ones, but too few who say boldly with Jabez, "Oh that thou wouldest bless me and enlarge my border" (1 Chron. 4:10 *RSV*), or with the aging Caleb, "Give me this mountain."

Someone has suggested strong leaders are scarce because our society no longer knows what leadership is. Who or what is a leader? The recent flurry over concepts such as authority, **elders, chief shepherd and so forth hasn't cleared the air as much as some had hoped. Some congregation members want** leaders to be forthright, standing fearlessly against the majority when necessary. Others prefer someone skilled in handling interpersonal relationships, thus keeping conflict in the church to a minimum.

Some people want a leader who will accept responsibility readily and move toward the cutting edge of society in ideas and practice. Others heartily agree — as long as they don't have to share the responsibility of being part of the cutting edge. Some want leaders who are able to share the emotions, hurts and burdens of those to whom they minister; others want leaders who mind their own business.

A *Time* essay (July 1974) points to reasons leadership has become unattractive in our society. First, institutions have changed in ways that leaders cannot always grasp. "Churches have been dramatically altered by internal disputes over questions of social activism, morals and even creed. Educators have grown uncertain about the social and intellectual purposes of education." As a result of such changes, leaders are made increasingly naked and vulnerable. People become skeptical of them. And if leaders don't know for sure where they're going, their followers feel uncertain also and pull back.

The essay adds that some of the people with leadership potential aren't around because they may have exhausted themselves during the protest movements of the sixties. I imagine some are now marching to the beat of a different drummer. Maybe even beating a drum elsewhere.

According to the *Time* writers, leadership is also unattractive because of the tremendous and complicated demands made on leaders. Few persons can reasonably accept such high expectations and remain whole. So they duck into some other type of work where the demands on them are less.

Years ago high school graduates were pushed into adulthood with the words of Longfellow's lines ringing in their ears: "Lives of great men, all remind us/We can make our lives sublime,/And departing leave behind us/Footprints in the sands of time."

Today these words have a faintly sentimental, almost maudlin, sound. Who wants to make life sublime? Who wants to leave footprints in the sands of time? Most people have too much to do now to think of leaving behind a reminder for the next generation.

Yet that's my point. Our generation probably wasn't concerned enough about providing role models (footprints) for the generation which got turned off in the sixties. Unless we can impress this generation that leaving footprints is more important than leaving large estates, the leadership crisis will only get worse.

Needed:
A capacity
for outrage

44

Katie: *I'm such a sissy. When it comes to standing up and being willing to be counted on some issue, I can always find an excuse not to be there.*

You: *But look at all the nice articles you write about nonviolence and peacemaking.*

Katie: *Yes, the words are fine, but peacemaking takes more than words. I rarely get so upset about some issues, that I would invest more than words.*

You: *You mean that?*

For years I have listened to discussions of the incident in Acts 15:39 in which Paul and Barnabas have a "sharp contention" whether John Mark shall accompany them. Their opinions clash so harshly they part company.

Some contemporary friends of Paul attempt to explain the disagreement away as a mild argument which author Luke overstated. To others, it becomes a vague embarrassment, for surely a man of Paul's stature wouldn't stoop to controversy or to letting his feelings show; far better if these verses were struck from the Holy Writ.

Why are some Bible readers reluctant to accept that Paul was a human being with feelings, sometimes negative ones? Probably because they have been taught that the Christian is slow to anger, never gets upset by circumstances and never causes trouble through disagreement. Praise is heaped upon those who are even-tempered, passive and calm, or who at least never show they're upset or disturbed.

As a result of this emphasis, some Christians believe that confrontation of any kind is bad, and that to let one's feelings show is out of order. Who has not sensed in a congregational meeting or small group meeting the fear those present have of opening up to one another, or, if someone does, the reluctance to let that person continue? The main goal seems to be to avoid a show of strong feeling, either negative or positive. As Bruce Larson suggests in *Ask Me to Dance*, in a discussion of the church as a celebrating community, insecurity in the face of hostility forces members to quench any sign of confrontation rather than let it out where they can deal with it.

Yet here's the problem. On the one hand the church encourages meekness, subordination and passivity. Yet at the same time I find the church perplexed by the widespread apathy of its members to the serious spiritual and social issues confronting church and society. Christians, like anyone else, have little capacity for outrage. Drug addiction, violence, rape, murder, racial prejudice, war, poverty, pornography, corruption at many levels of government, an over-abundance of X-rated movies, growing alcoholism, highway slaughter, epidemic proportions of venereal disease, all get a shrug of the shoulder: Let the authorities take care of it.

Consider a hypothetical case of a neighbor who is being harassed by another neighbor. How much would it take for the average Christian to become involved in their squabble? How many of the following factors would have to be present in the situation before he or she would step in: physical violence? extreme poverty? sickness? being a member of a minority race? being a widow or elderly? having a mentally retarded or physically handicapped child? being unemployed? being a member of the same church or denomination?

Harvey Cox, in *On Not Leaving It to the Snake*, points out that apathy is the key form of sin in today's world; it never was pride and rebellion. The church has come to believe that anger, insubordination and protest are never expressions of the gospel. The key qualities of a saint are accepted as being deference, submission and passivity. Pride and rebellion belong to the sinner.

But it's the other way around, he writes. A human being is not a Prometheus who rebels against God, but a person who, from the fall, has let someone else make the decisions — the snake. Before Eve reached for the fruit, she had "already surrendered her position of power and responsibility over to one of the animals, the serpent, and let it tell her what to do." When apathy controls a person's life, he or she refuses to accept the full measure of pain of decision-making and of the temptations that go with the wielding of the power necessary to care for and love one another.

Has the church become so well conditioned to be nice that its capacity for outrage has been reduced to a weak whimper, limited to griping about the loud music of the organist, the long shaggy hair of the minister's son, or the rescheduling of a television show at the last minute?

When Paul contended with Barnabas, I believe he experienced the pain and also the temptations that accompany positions of responsibility and decision-making that Cox writes about. Paul was disturbed about young John Mark and he said so. Perhaps his outrage was unfounded, I don't know. But he took the risk of taking a stand, as he had at other occasions, such as his opposition to the immorality in the Corinthian church or his support of Christian liberty for the Galatians. He was angry — and I'll leave the question of sinning to God. Our concern should be to help believers break out of the apathy — to be angry and to sin not.

The art of shelving

45

Katie: *The church is asking for people to bring some food to the Penners. Mrs. Penner is sick. I'd sure like to help . . . but it doesn't make sense to take time to cook a meal for them when my own family hasn't had a square meal in weeks.*

You: *How does that figure?*

Katie: *Well, I really haven't got the time to do all the things I'd like to do. I'll just send a card and tell her I'm thinking and praying for her. That should help.*

You: *Yes, but a card isn't food on their table.*

Katie: *Nor mine.*

Towards the end of the school term, teachers witness the hasty revival of the ancient art of making excuses, or "alibiography." With remarkable finesse students set forth the reasons for not having made the grade:

"My mother had to write a letter to Grandma, and my term paper was the only paper in the house, so she used the back side of it. I guess it'll be two weeks before it comes back."

"You see, I have this double hernia in my legs, and any movement, even in my fingers, brings on acute pain. I just couldn't write the paper."

"I washed my hands last night, and I just couldn't do a thing with them."

The art of shelving responsibility was with us when Adam

complained to God that the woman he had been given persuaded him to eat the forbidden fruit. People are still getting diplomas in this ingenious craft. Although daily life doesn't require written tests and papers, here's how some respond to age-old situations to avoid personal involvement and confrontation:

To the man lying by the side of Main Street, wiped out by thieves, "My brother, I've got wonderful news for you. Christ is the answer to all your needs. Just trust him to provide."

To the woman taken in adultery: "We'll appoint a committee today to study your case and write a position paper."

To the widows in Dorcas's neighborhood: "We'll pray for you. We'll put you on our round-robin prayer list today."

To the conscientious Nathan who has tried to pinpoint a serious behavioral problem: "Sorry about that. I guess I didn't read my Bible long enough or pray hard enough. Better luck next time."

To Mary, sitting in a most unfeminine way at the feet of Jesus: "Doesn't she know that a woman's place is in the kitchen and not squatting on the floor? It's time for coffee and rolls to be served, and I know it's Mary's turn to do dishes — someone call her."

To the aging Simeon and Anna, after they saw the Christ-child: "You've had a mountaintop experience today! Now let's set up a shuffleboard court and a domino table for you in the outer courtyard of the temple where you'll have a wonderful opportunity to review your thoughts."

To the Father of the Prodigal Son: "It was Adam's fault your son landed in a pigpen, not your son's. He shouldn't be blamed for what he did. It was mostly his societal conditioning."

To the Samaritan woman at the well: "It won't matter to us if you women, blacks and Chicanos use this well to draw water from. We won't make an issue of it. We'll overlook it. We really like you, you know."

To Jesus after hearing the Great Commission: "Great,

Lord, great! We'll have a missions conference at once and get the word out."

Apathy, indifference and the unwillingness to see the real problems of our day are often cited as some of the biggest problems our society faces. Admittedly, life is complex and frightening, almost compelling people to withdraw to safe ledges where they won't have to bear the pain of responsible decision-making and involvement. To stay on that ledge, they only have to master six easy lessons:

1. Always identify yourself as someone spiritually involved in others' needs through prayer, Bible study, attendance at conferences and conventions. Is a person in physical or emotional pain? Then say, "I'll pray for you." Is a person hurting because of oppression due to race, sex, age or social status? Then mutter loudly so all can hear: "Why do people create problems out of nothing? Don't these people know God has a special place for each person? If each one would only accept it, they'd be happy." Such responses guarantee release from direct personal involvement.

2. Encourage corporate involvement. Form committees, boards, organizations and other kinds of groups whenever a problem arises. If "they" are involved, that's enough.

3. Gently but firmly keep the problem, whatever it may be, at the level of rhetoric. Stay with words, filibustering if necessary. Learn the jargon of involvement, for it makes you sound like an experienced person even if you aren't.

4. Insist that feelings are important. Wax eloquently about your strong feelings about unsaved heathen, ghetto conditions or lonely prisoners. State clearly that you are interested. Shake your head sadly from side to side when such subjects are brought up. Sentiment counts for much to keep you safe on a ledge, even if love may be what is needed.

5. If the foregoing doesn't work, you have yet another recourse — to simply ignore the problem and thereby deny its existence. Never read about anything that might bother you,

like famine or corruption in politics, or increases in drug or alcohol abuse. Simply insist it's all a myth.

6. The alibiographer has one final recourse to avoid decision-making. Most such people don't learn it until they become more practiced in the art. It's very subtle — just leave it all "in God's hands." If someone is bothered by the ecological problems, throw the Great Planet Earth back into God's ample lap. After all, it's his world. Would he let it run out of energy? Would he force his children to walk to work instead of ride? Why should we become concerned about God's problems? Let him take care of them.

The school in the art of shelving responsibility enrolls many students annually. It's probably the biggest degree-granting institution around.

The Fog Machine

46

Katie: *I can't figure out how submission and authority fit together. Blacks and women are told to submit, never the whites and the men, yet Christ did most of his preaching to men who were leaders, especially religious leaders — top brass.*

You: *If you'd quit calling them top brass, you might find you have the answer.*

Someone has turned on the Fog Machine.

The hazy white stuff is rolling through the ventilators, making visibility in theological corridors problematic.

In Ken Kesey's *One Flew Over the Cuckoo's Nest*, Chief Broom, the mental patient who pretends to be deaf and dumb to avoid contact with people, is convinced that Head Nurse uses secret tactics to control her ward in the mental hospital. When she wants to confuse the patients, she throws a switch in the Nurses Station which pours dense fog over the entire ward, making it impossible for anyone to see clearly. Then she has the patients in her power, he thinks.

I get the feeling Head Nurse has thrown a switch in the ward of conservative theologians. The clouds of fog are billowing down the halls, confusing the issues of authority and submission.

I hear people talking a lot about these two concepts. They are important Christian principles, they say. I nod my head.

Take submission, for example; it is a characteristic of the Christian. I nod again. Humility is a sign of strength. Not dishrag or floormat humbleness but deliberate yielding. By now my head is jerking furiously.

But as I keep nodding, I find out that while these spokespersons for submission agree that submission is for all Christians, some members of the fold, especially underlings, are expected to submit more than others. It reminds me of the definition of equality some people use: All people are equal, but some are more equal than others.

Then I edge closer to a group talking about authority and how important it is to have authorities in today's complex society. Again I start nodding. All authority is of God, including heads of state, church and home. I almost develop a forward whiplash.

But when the fog starts moving in, I find I have nodded agreement to some strangely worded syllogisms. Because all authority is God-given, and because God holds us responsible for the authority he has given us, it is important to zealously guard this trust of responsibility (read authority here), to hang onto it (by psychological force if need be — no Hitler tactics just yet), and even to demand headship as one's right in certain situations.

Consider a husband who, as head of the home, says to his wife before his boss comes to dinner, "Look, honey, if the boss makes a little play for you this evening, it's okay by me. It may get me a promotion and you a new washer and dryer." So because he is her authority and she wants to be obedient, she agrees to a little hanky-panky a la Abram and Sarah in the Old Testament. And she can quote it, chapter and verse.

Or, if the employer growls at his secretary as he comes in from lunch, "If anyone calls this afternoon, tell him I'm out. I don't want to be bothered," she has no alternative but to obey. He is her authority.

Or, if a missionary executive orders a transfer back home for a single missionary because she is becoming too threatening to male leaders in her work on the field (nationals are turning to her for advice instead of to them), she should submit without question even though she may have some sanctified views on the subject of missions also.

The Fog Machine operators are making basic laws where Christ never taught them. His basic teaching was allegiance first and foremost to God. Then he taught a self-giving love — a principle of mutual submission for all believers, not just those of a certain age, sex, color or social position. "Submitting yourselves one to another in the fear of God" could mean the bank manager submitting to the janitor and the moderator of the church submitting to an elderly widow's concern. And if two sanctified persons hold opposite opinions and both feel the other is wrong and neither can submit, both are wrong if there is no disposition to yield, writes Everett Lewis Cattell in *The Spirit of Holiness*.

Christ taught repudiation of the power-patterns of the world: "Blessed are the meek," "He that loses his life shall find it." He taught that taking on the role of a servant was the highest and most powerful kind of authority (Phil. 2:1-12).

Yet all these teachings become somewhat garbled when wives are encouraged to submit to their husbands to control them and husbands urged to exert scriptural-based authority to keep their wives in line. Pagan men knew they should rule their wives and pagan wives knew they had to obey — or else. But Paul was speaking to Christians and introducing a new concept to them — self-giving love.

Anna B. Mow states in *Say Yes to Life* that historically there is only one thing wrong with "Wives, obey your husbands." In a Christian marriage, a husband can never use this order on his wife. It is an admonition for her alone. The wife must choose it or it has no spiritual value or power. A husband cannot demand headship on scriptural grounds, though many men have used Scripture to support this position of authority for centuries. How is the husband the head of the wife? By being a servant as Christ was (Mk. 20:26-28).

Obedience and submission is always a voluntary choice in any situation. Headship always means servanthood. A Christian relationship should be an invitation to growth, but when one partner must always yield to the other, the situation becomes an invitation to remain a conniving child to gain advantage. Unfortunately some wives have remained children because their marriage is one in which only the husband has opportunity for growth.

I do wish someone would turn off the Fog Machine.

They and us

47

Katie: *They did it again —*
You: *Who did it again?*
Katie: *You know — they — whoever they is — the people who run everything.*

A volunteer public official in a nearby city was found guilty of violating the Kansas Open Meetings Law earlier this spring. Such cases are rare and may prove to become precedents. In this instance, a meeting at which decisions were made had been closed to the public. A concerned citizen took the matter to court.

In handing down his decision, the judge cited Watergate and Nuremberg as examples of what happens when government conducts business of the public behind closed doors. He blamed both the public and the news media for a situation in which the public is "breast-fed" by the media's interpretation of public meetings. The public is not interested enough to find out what is happening firsthand.

The woman's action in closing the meeting reflects a growing tendency for administrators to make decisions without input from people working under them, whether in business, education, government or the church. We live in a society which fosters rule from the top. This growing faith in decision by an authoritarian body prompted one church leader to warn evangelicals against drinking "too deeply at the fountain of authoritarianism." Such an attitude can result in paralysis when decisive action against sin and evil is needed. Hitler's Germany is often cited as an example of how even Christians obediently endorsed strong leadership instead of demanding righteous leadership.

Though we need strong leaders, are closed doors necessary in church work? Where closed doors are the rule in making decisions, what happens? The body soon divides into "they" and "us." "They expect us to support this new program without our knowing much about it." "They changed the starting time for the evening service and didn't ask our opinion."

"They" becomes a nameless ominous power sitting on some ecclesiastical throne dispensing orders without feeling any emotion. "They" always expect everyone to fall in line without questions. Frequently the underlying feeling is "They didn't communicate with us about that matter. They made the decision alone without us. They don't trust us."

Decisions behind closed doors make those who had no part in them feel like outsiders, for closed doors are a form of power. Consciously or subconsciously the key in the lock represents an unwillingness to submit decision-making to persons of lesser maturity in case they may misunderstand a decision, misinterpret it, or if given a chance to decide, even reverse the expected decision.

Closed doors become the pattern when the final decision on programs and budgets becomes more important than the process of building unity within the body of Christ. Achieving consensus with a large group is a long and painful process. It takes time and effort. It requires much forbearance and concern for persons with strong opposing views. Because church members, like most people, are busy people, decision by a small administrative group makes more sense and even seems more biblical.

I am troubled, however, that many of our young people in

the church have never witnessed the emergence of a major decision on some doctrinal or ethical issue by consensus. I believe a person learns most about being a member of the body of Christ when he or she is involved in the emotions accompanying decision-making and not only the final decision.

Part of the reason for the interest of young adults in communes and house churches is the desire to become involved in decisions which concern them, whether trivial or major. They are looking for fellowship, not merely fellowship meetings. They refuse to call sitting together for an hour on Sunday mornings fellowship, for the Bible speaks not of "them" and "us," but of one body, one people, who are interdependent, interrelated and serving one another as they serve the Lord.

There is only "us" when members of the family of God teach and admonish one another (Col. 3:16), comfort one another (1 Thess. 4:18), are subject to one another (Eph. 5:21), bear one another's burdens (Gal. 6:2), and instruct one another (Rom. 15:14).

When the general trend shifts toward authoritarianism, the church of Jesus Christ has two responsibilities: (1) to keep doors flung wide open when decisions are being made which involve the members, and (2) to encourage all members to enter those doors and become part of the process of making decisions. Too many Christians enjoy the comfort and security of being on the sidelines where they won't be forced to sort through issues and make decisions.

Both actions require humility and willingness to learn from the other person. "They" becomes "we" and fellowship results.

A piece
of the rock

48

Katie: *How can I decide what aspects of church work to put my energies into?*

You: *Well, what kind of talents do you have? What are your interests?*

Katie: *Should I decide according to my talents, according to the needs in the church, or according to what I think is God's will for me?*

I asked a church member what he thought of the work of several of the denominational church boards. He shrugged. I added more information. I meant boards like missions, education, publications and so forth.

He smiled apologetically. His shoulders shifted again. He had no opinion. Those slightly visible pockets of ecclesiology which stuffed his Sunday bulletin or mailbox with literature had no reality for him. Out there, somewhere, in some distant office, were some boards with executive secretaries and book-keepers and secretaries. He accepted their necessity as he did those in the local church. They were leading someone somewhere. But he felt no close ties with them. They had not captured his spiritual imagination. Unlike the many policy holders of the well-advertised insurance company, he did not own a piece of this rock.

His lack of knowledge about and interest in the work of the

church as it is done by boards and committees is a concern of
church leaders. They want all members of a congregation to be
the people of God and the body of Christ. Too many like my
friend create a lopsided structure.

For some reason, some people get caught up in the work of
the church early in life and hang on until they die. They know
they are part of a people-of-God movement. They have seen
something happening. They know their contribution counts. It
fits in.

But others, like my friend, feel apart. They are faithful
church attenders. They may even be quite active as individuals
in some type of Christian work outside the church, but if asked,
they probably say they feel their support coming mostly from
God, only occasionally from a congregation, rarely from a
committee. They stand apart from a big part of what constitutes church work.

One church leader suggests the reason for this lack of
involvement in church programs may be that leaders are asking
the wrong questions. They should be asking "What does the
Lord require of you?" Instead they ask "What does humankind
need?" Although some might argue the questions are basically
the same, closer examination shows the second question focuses
on humankind. Which of humankind's numerous needs should
have first claim on the financial and personnel resources of the
church? Needs of body or spirit? If this can be determined, the
usual result is an emphasis on programs to meet those needs,
which in turn creates a need for people to fill the positions
created by these programs.

Programs need people. They swallow them whole to keep
the program going. Sunday school teachers, nursery helpers,
ushers, musicians, deacons — where are you? Occasionally I
feel the church will collapse unless each position has a candidate
and substitute.

If a congregation asks seriously "What does the Lord want
of us?" their concern will shift to making Christ and the vision
of the kingdom of God central. The function of the body of

Christ (and its boards and committees) will shift to helping each member be obedient to fulfilling God's plan for his or her life. The responsibility of boards will be to sponsor persons rather than programs. They will spend most of their energies helping each person find his or her gift of the Spirit and use it both within and without the church.

At this point I understand my opinionless friend. If I felt a call to work in evangelism or to promote social justice, I would feel little ownership in a congregation whose committees were pleading only for song leaders or Sunday school teachers. I'd want a place where I could fit in with my gifts, yet the committees would be looking for people to meet the needs of their programs, and if I weren't busy, I would get conscripted into service.

What a difference it would make if each church member were asked at a regular small group meeting, "What are your needs and concerns as a member of the local school board or as a businessperson? How can we, your fellow Christians, help you become an effective witness there?" Such words might shock at first, especially if this were the only program for the year. But eventually more people would feel they owned a piece of the rock and were part of the board of Christ, even if their names were not listed in a church directory of committees.

Wheels
and pyramids

49

Katie: *It's as if overnight everyone in the church is talking about power. The church has been politicized.*
You: *Well, even Christ talked about power.*
Katie: *Yes, but he talked about it in terms of servanthood. Servanthood was the way to power.*
You: *Anything wrong with power?*
Katie: *Not with power — power's probably amoral — but with the misuse and abuse of power. Power is another way sin can enter the community of saints.*

The prophet Ezekiel saw "a wheel within a wheel a-rolling, way up in the middle of the sky." If he were living today, I think he would be seeing pyramids within pyramids, way down in the middle of the church. I'm not thinking of stone structures, but the kind built by stepping on the shoulders of another person.

My problem appears in wholesome statements like this: "The Christian is committed to molding his or her life to Christ's. We are to follow his style of leadership. This means washing another's feet, laying down one's life for his friends, and loving one's enemies." These words sound like good evangelical language. In essence, they say we believe the Christian life is one of voluntarily relinquishing control, or servanthood.

Yet I hear people talking more about power than about servanthood. It comes out in expressions like "Top Brass, VIP, Head Honcho, the denominational chain of command" — spoken with or without grimaces and chuckles. Clout is another popular word. "Let's get so-and-so to do it, for he has clout," or "I couldn't get this idea through, because so-and-so has more clout than I have." No one talks about having more servanthood than the next person, or even wanting more servanthood!

Power is the ability to exercise control over the behavior and thinking of other people. Christ said that to have true power, his followers should be willing to be powerless with the powerless, to wash their feet if necessary. But servanthood, or washing feet, to some groups of people, especially the "little people," denotes a place of inferiority, which they have already involuntarily assumed at the bottom of the pyramid. Their shoulders are hurting from people stepping on them. They ask how you can become a suffering servant if you are already suffering because you are at the bottom? Can power be given up by anyone other than the one who has it? And who has it? They don't.

Minorities say the whites have power; the poor think the rich have it; employees think employers have it; laity thinks clergy and professionals in church have it; developing nations think the industrialized nations have it. When farm prices are low, the farmers haven't got it; and when criticism of the President runs high, he hasn't got it either.

Voluntary submission to one another, or true servanthood, is a stance freely chosen as a response to a situation in which one might have elected to be served instead of serving. Servant-hood seems to include deliberate self-limitation, an awareness of another person's need, and an ability and readiness to meet that need. Christ saw the disciples had dirty feet after tramping in the dust, so he picked up the towel and basin and washed them. He destroyed the pyramid and put everyone on an equal basis.

I see some real problems in reconciling power and servant-hood, however. I ask the same question as John Richard Burkholder in *Continuity and Change*: "It would seem on the one hand that the stance of subordination, submission and servant-hood would lead to utter renunciation — a complete relinquish-ment of power. But then what about institutions, about church organizations, about social and political action — all the mani-fold forms of power that are an inevitable part of our world? Just quoting Luke 22:25 does not take us very far."

How does a professional church leader become a servant when he or she is paid to keep things moving? Does servant-hood mean the employer sharpens pencils and empties waste-baskets? Can a congregation take the stance of a servant, for example, by giving up control of church buildings to uses other than those listed in the church bulletin — a day care center, for instance? Might laying down your life mean a husband's giving up the right to climb the career ladder for the sake of his family? Might it also mean that the body of Christ would have to eradicate its hierarchies to reveal a visible servanthood?

I heard of a church leader who gave up a position on a committee to allow a woman with interest in the field, but little experience, a chance to serve. He had the right to the position because of long years of dedicated work in the area. But he gave it up. Was this servanthood or foolishness? Was this true power?

Did Christ mean that wherever a little pyramid is being constructed of human beings, someone should surrender con-trol if that control is more important than Christ's love?

Clearly, Christ prefers a flat terrain to pyramids.

The light touch

50

Katie: *I dread the fall and winter months — getting schedules lined up, rushing about to meetings, trying to fit work, family and church into a neat package — it never stays that way.*

You: *Well, if you had your priorities straight, you wouldn't have a problem.*

Katie: *Priorities indeed!*

The other day as I was rushing between buildings on the college campus, the wind turned on me suddenly. Like a faithful dog unexpectedly snarling at his master, cold vicious blasts hurried the leaves into their corners and me to the shelter of my office.

Yes, it was fall. Though I wait for it, I don't like to admit it has come until I have turned on the furnace and checked the antifreeze in the car radiator. Tearing off the August calendar page means the beginning of fall and also the beginning of a new year like January 1 never has.

Though some brave individuals bound into September refreshed, re-tanned and re-vitaminized, others step over into the threshold with tippy-toe feelings, wondering what the stepped-up schedule of winter will bring this time. Ulcers? Headaches? Pain in the neck? Insomnia? Irritability? Indigestion? Or that general weariness which encases the body like a coat of molten lead? Where does strength for September come from for the person who feels as if he or she is living in a jet plane which hasn't been pressurized?

Part of the shift to fall includes children returning to school. Community programs and events move into visibility again. People move out of summer hibernation to find their place in the action of church life as committees and boards set forth their programs.

Each new fall I wonder again what it would be like if an entire congregation took several days, or even weeks, to answer the question: "What would we like to see happen in our congregation this winter?" Would they find answers, or is the average church member already so far removed from ultimate goal-making that this question is pertinent only to pastors and boards?

In churches where leadership is centralized in boards and committees, the usual pattern for planning is for these few people to do some quick brainstorming. If the committee members are typical, they adopt one of several approaches: If what happened last year in their area of concern was fairly successful, they decide to continue or to expand last year's program. If it wasn't, they check around for innovative programs being conducted in other churches and say, "Let's give it a try here also." This is the expected procedure, the goal of which is success. Whatever that means.

If they are not the average committee, they will make a study of existing needs in the congregation and come up with a program to meet that particular need. The difference between the two approaches is that with the first one people are urged, prodded and pushed to fit themselves into the needs of the program as planned. The people who have their arms twisted to take part are the ones who lose their wind very soon.

With the second approach, the program is adjusted to meet the needs of the people, because the committee knows people are more important than programs. This approach, however, is not as popular as the first because it lacks the security of tradition. It runs the risk of failure.

Behind the scenes, deep down in the hearts of many members, one senses a desire to see the Holy Spirit working in greater power, yet this desire is unexpressed out of fear of being labeled a radical. So the Holy Spirit is not given room to operate or even credited with doing much in the church. Instead, *Robert's Rules of Order*, constitutions, statistics and accounts of "how other churches successfully did the job" replace the spiritual weapons of faith, truth and prayer.

Meetings are begun with Scripture reading and prayer, and thereafter scriptural principles are laid to rest for the rest of the meeting. Self-sacrifice, cross-bearing, finding the hard and narrow road all yield to an insistence on security and traveling a superhighway with clear road signs. Always a congregation or committee is expected to be able to predict the outcome of any action instead of relying on the vagaries of an unpredictable Spirit. Leaders are not required to have a deep spiritual experience — only the ability to manage large groups of people so that they feel good and to keep congregations awake for thirty minutes.

There is no emphasis on congregation members becoming seriously involved with Christ's witness in the world. Call it the light touch, if you will, which means simply that everyone is expected to do his or her fair and equal share of the Lord's work, none of which should take too much of one's time or demand too great a commitment. It does not require persons to explore and use their gifts. It asks only that they give some time briefly and occasionally in an area in which they may have little interest. Democratic and organized.

The light touch or token involvement has penetrated nearly every area of church life under the guise of getting more people involved or making sure no one person carries too heavy a load. How unlike Isaiah, who, when the Lord said, "Who will go for me?" didn't respond with, "But it's not my turn until the second Monday in June," but with "Here am I, send me."

Strength for the individual member comes from knowing one's gift and using it. The service may be difficult but it will be a joy. Lists on the bulletin board are not always of the Lord's design. Nor attempts to keep positions filled on a rotating basis.

Strength for the congregation comes with helping each member find that gift. God left no one out when he gave gifts to the church. With each person aware of his or her gift and using it, fall is never merely a rescheduling of last year's best programs.

Let's try
at least
two cheers

51

You: *Come on, how about a little more enthusiasm?*
Katie: *Who me? You know I couldn't — that's not me.*
You: *Sure you can — no one will mind.*
Katie: *No one but me. I'd look ridiculous whooping it up.*

I have attended more basketball games after forty than before, partly because my son was becoming interested in the game and partly because I was curious about this sport which so captivates Americans. In Canada, I grew up with hockey as the main winter sport.

As the result of my limited exposure to the game, I have seriously asked myself what it would take to persuade me, a middle-aged mother of four, to jump up and down, shriek, scream and clap my hands as the fortunes of my favorite team rise and fall. Probably quite a bit.

I have come to the conclusion that middle-age inhibitions are hard to overcome. It is hard to become an exuberant fan when one is wearing bifocals and seriously considering jogging as a necessity.

Although I enjoy watching a game of basketball, I have not been conditioned to whoop and holler any more than I have been conditioned to shout "Amen" and "Hallelujah" at a church service. I find the one as hard to do as the other.

Many of our group responses, such as cheering at a game,

are learned responses. Young children easily learn to respond openly to the cheerleaders, even as they soon learn that in a service any kind of overt enthusiasm is out of place. Though we wouldn't want the rowdy atmosphere of a ball game at a service, we have conditioned people not only not to get involved but to be rigidly silent.

In Sunday school, students are trained from childhood up to accept quietly what the teacher offers. Somewhere the idea has been nurtured that the church is not the place to ask questions, even very troubling questions about the faith. So in numerous Christian educational settings, teachers struggle to make adult classes into groups of enthusiastic, involved believers.

At congregational meetings, the members are conditioned to avoid conflict at all price in the mistaken assumption that the absence of tension is the real goal of the church instead of the spiritual maturity of its members. Christians sometimes are so anxious to avoid any kind of confrontation that they act like strangers with one another. They say what is expected of them.

This also holds true for prayer meetings. After having been connected with Christian work for several decades, I grieve as I hear people pray about everything except what really concerns them. They pray through short and long prayer lists and all around the world, but their personal relationships and problems are disregarded. Maybe this is conditioning. Maybe it is already a sickness.

It adds up to the fact that we have been conditioned to reserve our enthusiasm and spontaneity for athletic events and our passive, indifferent response to God — not the best arrangement. We need enthusiasm and a willingness to share ourselves with others in the church fellowship. We need people who are willing to become more open about their spiritual pilgrimage and to articulate their relationship to God and the church. By this I don't mean more opportunity for canned "testimonies" — the kind which are many days or years old and are taken down from the mind's shelf and dusted off for each occasion.

We need to learn to talk about what Christ means to us in ordinary everyday terms when we are together as believers. Unless this happens, I doubt whether we can talk about him to unbelievers.

A beginning might be to learn to talk together about the morning sermon in small groups. I can imagine that this is what happened when Jesus, the Apostle Paul or Peter preached. People stopped to ask questions and to discuss what had been said. Of course, some preachers might feel a little threatened by such an approach. It has long been accepted that the minister has the last word. It might be equally threatening to some laypersons who find their pews comfortable and their own silence golden. They fear sharing their dearth. Unfortunately, it is most difficult to wean people away from what appears to be the safe pattern of church involvement.

As I said, bifocals and jogging don't like change, but let's try at least two cheers.

Peace
be with you

52

Katie: *I feel a little funny going to a Catholic service. Mennonites and Catholics haven't had much to do with each other for a long time.*

You: *Why judge them before you've been with them?*

Katie: *I'm not judging them. It's just that Protestants and Catholics don't usually have anything in common, so why go? My neighbors wouldn't understand.*

"We'd never have anything like that in one of our churches," commented my son from his 14-year-old perspective. We had visited another church which emphasized openness and celebration. He liked it.

The 90-year-old sanctuary breathed orthodoxy and tradition from every weathered brick, every stained-glass window, and every well-worn pew in its structure. Yet this image was shattered when the service began. At the front, a group of young guitarists led the opening song, "Just a closer walk with God," the words of which were projected onto a homemade screen.

The sanctuary was capable of holding about 500 people if the entire floor had been filled with pews. But it wasn't. In front of the altar, a large rug-covered empty space stared at me. The pews were arranged in a U-shape around this space. Unusual, I thought, until I saw the reason for this strange arrangement later on. This was essential living space.

A large brightly lettered poster greeted the congregation: "We are an Easter people with a Christmas God." Another large poster nearby shouted, "Christ has died, Christ is risen, Christ will rise again." From the ceiling, outshining the stained-glass windows, hung other posters in brilliant coloring and contemporary design declaring "Faith—Yes," "Trust in God," and "Color my world hope." I am used to bold posters and pictures at a missionary conference, but not usually for something as ordinary as a Sunday morning service.

The congregation, composed mostly of young families or young people, were dressed casually and comfortably. I noted numerous pairs of jeans. When the pews filled up, latecomers found spots around the back and sides, some standing.

Two persons from the congregation read Scripture passages after which we listened to a sermon on spiritual preparation for Easter. Lent is a time for rebuilding our zeal for our Father's house, a time for renewal. "We are the temple of God in the world — the revelation of Christ to the world," said the speaker. Fasting and prayer are important, so we can get outside of ourselves and so Christ can get to us, we were told.

Two prayer weekend retreats at a nearby camp were announced. Members were encouraged to join a study group dealing with the life of Christ according to Matthew's Gospel, but not "just as a historical critter, but as One who is alive now."

Opportunity was given to share experiences with Christ during the past week. One young woman related how Christ is often considered an absurdity in today's world, yet an awareness of Christ had helped her to overcome a temporary illness sufficiently to meet a commitment to share the living reality of Christ in her marriage with a discussion group.

Without a printed order of service, we could only wait expectantly for what was to come. No one seemed concerned if nothing was happening at every moment. After we had waited for a few moments for the children to come up from the lower auditorium, the congregation was instructed to give each other the sign of peace. Suddenly the empty space in front of the altar came alive with people moving about shaking hands, greeting each other, often with a kiss and the words, "Peace be with you."

In front of me a young husband and wife looked each other briefly in the eyes before clasping hands, murmuring "Peace" and kissing. I liked that. Beside them their little five-year-old boy wriggled, toying with a paper cup, half-filled with dirt in which a wheat seed had been planted. The couple turned to greet us and others near them. So unaccustomed to this openness, I realized later I had not greeted those behind me.

At the communion service, the participants moved to the altar to receive the bread and the wine, filling the empty area again. Others sang communion hymns. It was a different way of serving communion.

Early in my church experience, the congregation used the common cup, a great glass or silver goblet filled with wine. In time it was replaced by the more sanitary plastic cuplets. I have seen the deacons pass around great crusty loaves of bread, broken aesthetically in the middle, so each participant could pluck a morsel from the generous interiors. But I have also partaken of neat cubes of Kleenex-like material, devoid of all crusts, which collapsed between my fingers when I picked it up. I have been served communion by preachers in plaid suits while sitting in my pew. I have watched deacons with serious mien, often with bald pate and in black suits, march up and down the aisles in perfect step, carrying their silver plates. On rare occasions young men and women in ordinary school clothes served the elements.

What matters most is not the outward form but to see oneself as part of a community of forgiven sinners, who sense their unworthiness but also the joy of being joined in fellowship with the Lord and other believers. It means being willing to pass the peace.

As we left the church that Sunday morning, we received a

bulletin with the week's announcements printed on a discarded freight waybill. Why not, I asked myself. Bulletins usually get thrown out soon anyway.

As we drove away I took a last look at the old building. At one time it probably sheltered a prosperous congregation. Now it edged the ghetto, or better, the ghetto edged it. At one time the service in this Catholic church was probably rigidly orthodox and liturgical. Today it risked breaking tradition to bring a more meaningful sense of Christ's body to the families who call it their spiritual home.

About a block away I noticed a Protestant church, also beautifully old with a stained-glass window and high-reaching spires. But it was empty during this Lenten season.

What if . . . ?

53

Katie: *Is there hope things will ever change?*
You: *Always!*
Katie: *Tell me more. . . .*
You: *All we need is dreamers like Joseph. . . .*

In August Kansas had 13 days with a temperature over 100 degrees. September follows the same pattern. Each day the weary earth cringes under the blowtorch rays of the sun. Withered leaves drift to the ground. The grass crumbles under my feet.

At night as the fan drones, pushing dead air over my bed and body, I wait for sleep. Then I discover the wonderful game of "What if . . .?" Each new "What if" rushes past me with a new surge of night air.

I remember I forgot to pick up a church bulletin. What if church bulletins were abolished and members attended only what they remembered from spoken announcements? Which activities would be attended regularly? What would die out by default?

What if every letter in my mailbox for the next month was a personal letter, and the mailman never had to carry junk mail anymore? Who would rejoice more, he or I?

What if all copiers and duplicators were raptured to wherever such prolific beasts of burden belong and life slowed down to a normal paper chase again?

What if every family in the congregation subscribed to a family devotional guide and used it daily, and then got so excited about learning to know God together, they had no time for "Little House on the Prairie" or "Monday Night Football"?

What if inner growth were possible without attending distant seminars, workshops, conventions and retreats and thrived through the use of the spiritual gifts present in the members of the local congregation?

What if Bible studies were the best attended meetings of the week?

What if all adult Bible classes became intergenerational, and Grandpa, 79, got a chance to discuss his tastes in music and hairstyles with Betsy, 19?

What if Mennonites agreed to agree on the mode of baptism and the issue never came up again in any formal conversation between these groups? What would historians have to write about in the future?

What if every activity announced or advertised as "timely, informative, exciting and challenging" was timely, informative, exciting and challenging? And if it wasn't, what if the person who made the statement grew a Pinocchio-type nose at once? What if meetinghouses also developed huge wooden proboscises at odd places, like the front vestibule, if the church bulletin said, "A warm welcome awaits you here," and the welcome was only a tepid gesture? What if every public relations cover-up statement by a church-related institution grew a long nose on every member of the department if they ever spoke "evangelistically"?

That's enough "what ifs" to awaken me to full alert. The temperature has cooled to 85 degrees at one in the morning. But now my game has become more interesting than sleep.

What if the Apostle Paul had had a wife who was a better speaker and writer than he, and ten children, four of whom were daughters who prophesied like those of the gentle Philip?

What if nobody had to feel uncomfortable again about

being timid or nonassertive or unfulfilled or unsuccessful? In other words, what if it was okay not to be okay the way everyone else thinks you should be okay?

What if the elderly developed such an attractive image because of their prestige and multitudinous opportunities for service that the middle-aged started to bleach their hair gray to look older?

What if every person who feels secure and important because of education, social class, wealth, sex or race, rather than because of the contribution he or she makes to the community of believers, spent a day in the skin of a person who feels he or she isn't receiving any fringe benefits because he or she is on the fringe?

What if we celebrated the Lord's Supper by sitting in small circles, so that we could talk with one another and look into each other's face instead of sitting so we study the grain in the wood on the backside of the pews, the size of the shirt collars or the skill of the zipper seamstress?

What if church members became so enthusiastic about the mission of the church that the treasuries of all boards overflowed and the staff members had to work overtime to find ways of spending the money instead of working overtime to stretch available funds?

What if the peace-loving Mennonites became well known for their practice of love, honesty, servanthood, peacemaking and evangelism instead of their rhetoric?

What if . . . what if . . . On that one, I drop off to sleep.

Thoughts
for Advent

54

Katie: *Christmas means something different each year.*
You: *Why shouldn't it? You're not the same person you were last year or even the year before.*

Katie: *Christmas for a time was mostly pressure — to do and to go and to give and to make. As I get older, that pressure eases, but a different one takes its place, and I can't quite put my finger on what it is.*

The day after Thanksgiving we went shopping. Every trace of the November holiday had been erased as if by a giant mop. Instead, the aisles and shelves were jammed with stock for the Christmas market. The overload seemed to be mostly trinkets and gadgets — items to hang on walls or push into corners or rest on shelves. Or to throw into the Salvation Army drop box after a suitable period of waiting.

A young woman bumped into me with her cart, mumbling an apology about having to get her shopping done. Her expression seemed half-dazed and half-resentful, as if someone had come from behind without warning and pushed her headlong into the season.

I saw myself in that young woman. Like many others, I've rushed through the Advent season like a tourist who wants only to be able to say "I was there." Nothing more. I know I've gone through most emotions in relation to Christmas, including hers. As a child I experienced the unspeakable ecstasy of waiting for the most wonderful day of the year. As a young person, the feeling changed to the different joy of going back to the place I was eager to get away from a few months earlier.

As a young homemaker, I found myself trapped by the rigid demands laid upon all Christian homemakers, or so it seemed to me. Each Christmas preparation had to be equal to or greater than the sum of all previous Christmas preparations. The result: batches of cookies, cakes, fruitcake, candy, popcorn. Christmas dresses for every daughter, new shirts for the men. Gifts for family, friends, relatives. Gift exchanges. Cards. Banquets, programs and more programs and concerts. And visiting and family dinners.

Later on, as Christians began to protest the commercialization of Christmas, I added my voice to "Keep Christ in Christmas." Then still later, I felt indignant at the weak attempts to do so when I saw a Scripture verse stamped on a gift item or card, whether it was a 25-cent paper-knife or an expensive vase. How important it had seemed to convince God we were on his side.

As I examined my attitudes more thoroughly, I felt uncomfortable at the emphasis on the details of the birth of Christ. Why did we worship a baby and not an adult? What other great person's birthday is celebrated with baby pictures?

I have cringed at the sincere attempts to make Christmas functional in terms of the church budgets, attendance and witnessing. Why do children have to sing and speak lines they neither understand nor enjoy, but which are chosen for their adult "message"? Surely honest joy in the Lord is also a witness?

Recently I've been wondering at the joking apologies for Christmas activities that are not easily brought under the spiritual umbrella, like spending Christmas Day watching football. Yes, our affluence has made us tolerant of many things for Christ's sake. If the times demand them, it seems best to adjust and give the Lord equal time and finances — a football game for each worship service and a dollar for each dollar spent for gifts and fun.

As I approach this Christmas, I am not sure whether the more mature understanding I have of Advent is still riddled with blind spots. I think I have learned, not without emotional discomfort, that life doesn't stop if cards aren't sent out on time. I have learned that gift-giving, whether to family, friends, the needy or the church, can all be spiritual gifts if given as to the Lord. Attendance at programs, banquets and concerts can be selective. Some of these pressures are off.

But a new pressure has taken their place which I wish had been there long ago. I welcome it. The new pressure is simply wondering whether those of us who call ourselves Christians would know God without the support of these many programs and arranged fellowship. Do we know the reality of Christ's presence, day by day, moment by moment? Do we know him, the Christ?